INTERNATIONAL EXPRESSWAYS

$7·95

Rs. 215/-

ILO   National Project   MWD GOP)
Strengthening of Secretarial Training for Women
Room 804 Floor 8 State Life Building Blue Area
Islamabad, Telephone, Fax 051-826522

INTERNATIONAL EXPRESSWAYS

*Exercises in functions, topics and grammar
for interactive conversation practice*

Intermediate level

Steven J. Molinsky
and
Bill Bliss

Prentice Hall

New York   London   Toronto   Sydney   Tokyo

First published 1989 by
Prentice Hall International (UK) Ltd,
66 Wood Lane End, Hemel Hempstead,
Hertfordshire, HP2 4RG
A division of
Simon & Schuster International Group

© 1989 Prentice Hall International (UK) Ltd
Adapted from *ExpressWays* 3, © Prentice Hall Inc.

Printed and bound in Great Britain at the
University Press, Cambridge.

Library of Congress Cataloging-in-Publication Data

Molinsky, Steven J.
International expressways: exercises in
functions, topics and grammar for interactive
conversation practice / Steven J. Molinsky
and Bill Bliss.
p. cm.
Bibliography: p.
Includes index.
ISBN 0-13-472887-4 : $10.00 (est.)
1. English language — Textbooks for foreign
speakers. 2. English language — Conversation
and phrase books. I. Bliss, Bill. II. Title
PE1128.M677 1989
428.3'4 — dc19 88-38722

British Library Cataloguing in Publication Data

Molinsky, Steven J.
International expressways: exercises in
functions, topics and grammar for
interactive conversation practice.
1. Spoken English language — For
non-English speaking students I. Title
II. Bliss, Bill
428.3'4

ISBN 0-13-472887-4

---

1 2 3 4 5 93 91 91 90 89

CONTENTS

TO THE TEACHER

International ExpressWays is a fast-moving course in spoken functional English for adult and young-adult learners. It consists primarily of a collection of lively functional dialogues which can be practised and then extended and adapted, by means of illustrated cues and alternative key expressions given in an option box, to meet other situations.

This volume is intended for intermediate-level students who have been exposed to the essentials of grammar and who have already mastered the usage of English for everyday-life situations. The text builds upon and reinforces this foundation and prepares students for higher-level language skills required for effective interpersonal communication. *International ExpressWays* is organized functionally, while incorporating integrated coverage of grammar and topics.

THE DIMENSIONS OF COMMUNICATION: FUNCTION, FORM AND CONTENT

Some ELT texts present the functional syllabus by describing language use and listing sets of functional phrases. The exercises and activities that normally accompany these descriptions and lists usually occur in isolation, rather than being totally integrated into active conversational practice. In addition, traditional functional approaches usually do not give students intensive communicative practice using the correct grammatical forms that are required by particular functional language choices.

International ExpressWays, essentially, does not seek to provide students with background knowledge about language use. Rather, it provides dynamic practice that involves students in lively interactions based on the content of real-life contexts and situations. The functional syllabus is fully integrated into a complete conversational course in which students not only learn the various ways to express each function, but also intensively practise the grammatical forms required to turn functional expressions into effective communication in English.

Every unit offers students simultaneous practice with one or more functions, the grammatical forms needed to express those functions and the contexts and situations in which the functions and grammar are used. This 'tri-dimensional clustering' of function, form, and content is the organizing principle behind each lesson and the cornerstone of the *International ExpressWays* approach to functional syllabus design.

International ExpressWays offers a broad exposure to uses of English as an international language in a variety of relevant contexts: in community, academic, employment, home, and social settings. The characters portrayed are intended to represent people of different ages, ethnic groups, nationalities and occupations, interacting in situations in different international locations.

While some texts make a point of giving students a range of ways of expressing a function, from extremely polite to informal, we have chosen to take the middle ground and concentrate on those expressions that would most frequently occur in normal polite conversation between people in various settings. A variety of registers is offered, from the formal language someone might use in a job interview, with a customer, or when speaking with an authority figure, to the informal language someone would use when talking with family members, co-workers, or friends. Reference is made to American English, where expressions differ considerably. When appropriate, the text also presents students with alternative degrees of expressing a function, such as strength of disagreement and certainty or the directness of requests and advice.

A special feature of the programme is the treatment of discourse strategies. Students actively practise initiating conversations and topics, interrupting, hesitating, asking for clarification, and other conversation skills.

AN OVERVIEW

Guided conversations

Guided conversations are the dialogues and exercises that are the central learning devices in the programme. Each lesson begins with a model guided conversation that illustrates the use of one or more functions and the structures they require, all in the context of a meaningful exchange. Key functional expressions in the models are in bold-face type and are footnoted, referring students to short lists of alternative expressions for accomplishing the functions. In the exercises that follow, students create new conversations by placing new contexts, content, or characters into the framework of the model, and by using any of the alternative functional expressions.

'Now present your own conversations'

Each lesson ends with this open-ended exercise which offers students the opportunity to create and present original conversations based on the model and any of the alternative expressions. Students contribute content based on their experiences, ideas, and imaginations, while staying within the framework of the model.

   We should emphasize that the aim of each unit is to provide a measure of controlled practice with a dialogue and guided conversation exercises so that students can competently use functional expressions in creating their own original conversations.

Interchange

This activity, at the end of most units, offers students the opportunity to create and to present guided role plays. Each activity consists of a model that students can practise and then use as a basis for their original presentations. Students should be encouraged to be inventive and to use new vocabulary in these presentations and should feel free to adapt and expand the model in any way they wish.

Scenes and improvisations

These free role plays appear at intervals, offering review and synthesis of functions and conversation strategies which appear in the preceding units. Students are presented with scenes depicting conversations between people in various situations. They use the information in the scenes to determine who the people are and what they are talking about. Then, students improvise based on their perceptions of the scenes' characters, contexts, and situations.

   The purpose of these improvisations is to offer recombination practice that promotes students' absorption of the preceding units' functions and strategies into their repertoire of active language use.

Support and reference sections

International Expressways offers a number of support and reference sections:

* The contents provide an overview of the functions and conversation strategies in each unit.
* Each unit begins with a list of functional and grammatical contents.
* End-of-unit summaries provide complete lists of expressions for the functions and conversation strategies appearing in each unit.
* An inventory of functions and conversation strategies in the Appendix offers a comprehensive display of all expressions for the functions and conversation strategies in the text, and indicates the units in which the expressions appear.
* An index of functions and conversation strategies and an index of grammatical structures provides a convenient reference for locating coverage of functions and grammar in the text.

SUGGESTED TEACHING STRATEGIES

When you use *International ExpressWays*, we encourage you to develop approaches and strategies that are compatible with your own teaching style and needs and abilities of your students. While the programme does not require any specific method or technique in order to be used effectively, you may find it helpful to review and try out some of the following suggestions.

Guided conversations

- *Listening*. With books closed, students listen to the model conversation recorded on cassette.
- *Discussion*. Students discuss the model conversation: Who are the people? What is the situation?
- *Reading*. With books open, students follow as two students present the model.
- *Practice*. In pairs, small groups, or as a class, students practise the model conversation.
- *Alternative expressions*. Present to the class each sentence of the dialogue containing a footnoted expression. Call on different students to present the same sentence, but replacing the footnoted expression with its alternatives. (You can cue students to do this quickly by asking, 'What's another way of saying that?' or 'How else could he/she/you say that?')
- *Pair practice*. (optional) Pairs of students simultaneously practise all the exercises, using the footnoted expressions or any of their alternatives.
- *Presentation*. Pairs of students present the exercises, using the footnoted expressions or any of their alternatives. Before students present, set the scene by describing the characters and the context or ask the students to do this themselves.

'Now present your own conversations'

In these activities that follow the guided conversations at the end of each lesson, pairs of students should create and present original conversations based on the model and any of the alternative expressions. Encourage students to be inventive as they create their characters and situations. (You may want to assign this exercise as homework, asking students to prepare their original conversations, practise them the next day with another student, and then present them to the class. In this way, students can review the previous day's lesson without actually having to repeat the specific exercises already covered.)

Interchange

Students practise the model using the same steps listed above for guided conversations. Then pairs of students create and present original conversations using the model dialogue as a guide. Encourage students to be inventive and to use new vocabulary. (You may want to assign this exercise as homework, asking students to prepare their conversations, practise them the next day with another student, and then present them to the class.) Students should present their conversations without referring to the written text, but they should also not memorize them. Rather, they should feel free to adapt and expand them any way they wish.

Scenes and improvisations

Students should talk about the people and the situations, and then present role plays based on the scenes. Students may refer back to previous lessons as a resource, but they should not simply reuse specific conversations. (You may want to assign these exercises as written homework, asking students to prepare their conversations, practise them the next day with another student, and then present them to the class.)

You will notice that most functions and conversation strategies occur at several different points in the text. In this way, content is reviewed and expanded upon at regular intervals. Students may find it especially helpful to have frequent focused reviews of many of the alternative expressions for specific functions and conversation strategies. One useful technique is to ask a pair of students to present a model conversation from a previous lesson while other students listen with books closed. Stop the presentation after any line that contains a footnoted expression and ask different students to present the same line, but replacing the footnoted expression with its alternatives. (You can cue students to do this quickly by asking, 'What's another way of saying that?' or 'How else could he/she/you say that?')

In conclusion, we have attempted to offer students a communicative, meaningful, and lively way of practising the functions of English, along with the grammatical structures needed to express them competently. While conveying to you the substance of our textbook, we hope that we have also conveyed the spirit: that learning to communicate in English can be genuinely interactive, truly relevant to our students' lives and fun!

Steven J. Molinsky
Bill Bliss

A NOTE ABOUT USING THE FOOTNOTES

Here are the conventions that you will need to know in order to use the footnotes containing alternative expressions in each lesson.

1. In the model conversation, a bold-faced footnoted expression indicates that there are alternative ways of expressing this function. Sometimes this expression is an entire sentence and sometimes it is only a portion of a sentence.

2. ( ) indicates that the word or words are optional. For example, the footnote:
   I'm (very) sorry to hear (about) that. = I'm sorry to hear that.
   I'm very sorry to hear that.
   I'm sorry to hear about that.
   I'm very sorry to hear about that.

3. / indicates that the words on either side of the / mark are interchangeable. For example, the footnote:
   I don't/can't believe it! = I don't believe it!
   I can't believe it!

4. Sometimes the ( ) and / symbols appear together. For example, the footnote:
   I'm not (completely/absolutely) sure. = I'm not sure.
   I'm not completely sure.
   I'm not absolutely sure.

5. Sometimes the footnote indicates that an alternative expression requires a change in the grammar of the sentence. For example, the footnote:
   How about _____ing?   How about going shopping?
   Let's _____.   = Let's go shopping.
   What if we _____ed?   What if we went shopping?

6. (Am.E.) = American English usage.

Components of a lesson

A **model conversation** offers initial practice with the functions and structures of the lesson.

Key functional expressions are in bold-face type and are footnoted, referring students to a box containing alternative expressions for accomplishing the functions.

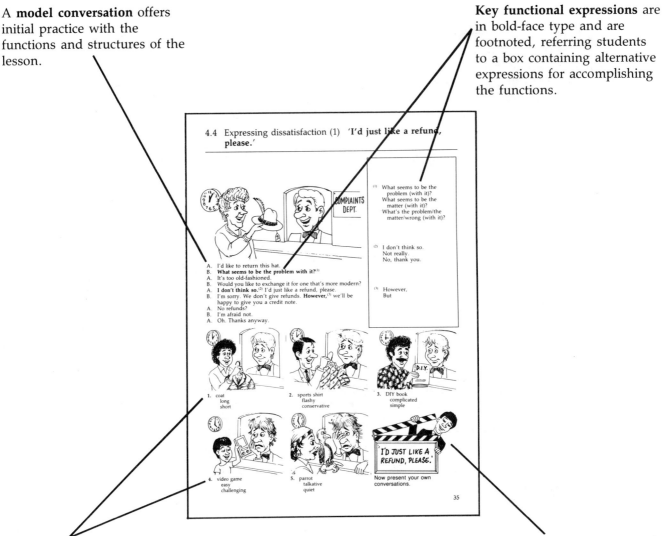

In the **exercises**, students create conversations by placing new contexts, content, or characters into the model, and by using any of the alternative functional expressions.

The **open-ended exercise** at the end of each lesson asks students to create and present original conversations based on the model and any of the alternative expressions.

For example:

Exercise 1 might be completed by placing the new exercise content into the existing model:

A. Would you like to eat at home or in a restaurant?
B. I think I'd prefer to eat at home. How about you?
A. Well, to be honest, I really don't feel like eating at home. I'd much rather eat in a restaurant. Is that okay with you?
B. Yes. We haven't eaten in a restaurant for a long time anyway.

Exercise 2 might be completed by using the new exercise content *and* some of the alternative functional expressions:

A. Would you prefer to swim in the sea or in the pool?
B. I think I'd like to swim in the sea. How about you?
A. Well, to be honest, I'm not really in the mood for swimming in the sea. I'd much rather swim in the pool. Is that okay with you?
B. Yes. We haven't swum in the pool for a long time anyway.

UNIT 1: MEETING AND LEAVE TAKING

1.1 *Meeting and greeting*
'I don't think we've met.'

1.2 *Introducing*
'Let me introduce my friend Paul.'

1.3 *Initiating a conversation*
'Excuse me, but don't I know you from somewhere?'

1.4 *Identifying*
'Guess who I saw yesterday!'

1.5 *Leave taking* (1)
'I think I should be going now.'

1.6 *Leave taking* (2)
'I've really got to go now.'

Summary

Simple present
Negative questions
Relative clauses with who/whose, one/ones
Simple past
Used to
Past continuous (— 'always')
Neither did I
Must (deductive)
Have to/must/am supposed to/have got to/had better/should

(1) My name is
     I'm

(2) Hello.

     [less formal]
     Hi.

     [more formal]
     How do you do?

(3) (I'm) pleased to meet you.
     (I'm) glad to meet you.

     (It's) nice to meet you.
     (It's) nice meeting you.
     (I'm) happy to meet you.
                        (Am.E.)

(4) How about you?
     What about you?
     And you?

Carmen   Kenji

A. I don't think we've met. **My name is**[1] Carmen.
B. **Hello.**[2] **I'm**[1] Kenji. **Pleased to meet you.**[3]
A. **Pleased to meet you,**[3] too. Where are you from?
B. Japan. **How about you?**[4]
A. I'm from Venezuela.

Tom   Carol

1. dancer
    English teacher

Eileen   Betty

2. 2C
    4D

Pedro   Nick

3. two months
    one year

Ted   Carl

4. Dr Murphy
    Dr Gold

Frank / Gloria

5. Accounting
Shipping

Linda / Bob

6. History
Chemistry

Jane / Sally

7. the morning shift
the night shift

Alan / Ruth

8. the bride's
the groom's

Steve / Judy

9. a lawyer
a journalist

Paul / Dave

10. rock
jazz

Donna / Martha

11. next month
any day now

Now present your own conversations.

1.2 Introducing 'Let me introduce my friend Paul.'

(1) How are you?

[less formal]
How are things?
How's it going?
How are you doing?
                    (Am.E.)

(2) Fine (thank you/thanks).
All right.
Okay.
Not bad.

(3) Let me introduce (you to)
I'd like to introduce (you to)
I'd like you to meet

[less formal]
This is

A. Hi! **How are you?**(1)
B. **Fine.**(2) And you?
A. **Fine, thanks.**(2) **Let me introduce**(3) my friend Paul.
B. Pleased to meet you.

1. my brother Tom

2. my sister Kate

3. my roommate, Peter

4. my English teacher, Mrs Simon

5. my fiancé, Steve Smith

Now present your own conversations.

4

1.3 Initiating a conversation
'Excuse me, but don't I know you from somewhere?'

A. **Excuse me,**[1] but don't I know you from somewhere?
B. No, I don't think so.
A. Yes. Don't you work in the bank in the High Street?
B. No, I'm afraid not. You must have me **confused**[2] with somebody else.
A. Oh, **I'm sorry.**[3] I must have made a mistake.

[1] Excuse me.
Pardon me. (Am.E.)

[2] confused
mixed up

[3] I'm sorry.
Excuse me. (Am.E.)

1.

2.

3.

4.

5.

'EXCUSE ME, BUT.....?'

Now present your own conversations.

Kathy Wilson
She saved my life when I almost drowned last year.

The Bradley twins
Their parents used to dress them alike all the time.

A. **Guess**[1] who I **saw**[2] yesterday!
B. Who?
A. Kathy Wilson!
B. Kathy Wilson? I don't think I remember her.
A. Oh, surely you do! She's the one who saved my life when I almost drowned last year.
B. Oh, of course. Now I remember her. How IS she?
A. **Fine.**[3]
B. Did she say much?
A. Not really. We just talked **for a minute.**[4] But it was really good to see her again.

A. **You won't believe**[1] who I **ran into**[2] yesterday!
B. Who?
A. The Bradley twins!
B. The Bradley twins? I don't think I remember them.
A. Oh, surely you do. They're the ones whose parents used to dress them alike all the time.
B. Oh, of course. Now I remember them. How ARE they?
A. **Fine.**[3]
B. Did they say much?
A. Not really. We just talked **for a moment.**[4] But it was really good to see them again.

[1] Guess	[2] saw	[3] Fine	[4] for a minute
You won't believe	ran into	He/she/they look/s	for a moment
	bumped into	well/okay/fine.	for a few minutes
			for a few seconds

1. Professor Kingston
He taught economics at college.

2. Mr and Mrs Larson
They used to live next door to us.

3. Miss Hubbard
Her car was always breaking down in front of our house.

4. The Bennetts
Their daughter sometimes baby-sits for us.

5. Lucy Crawford
She's the head of the Education Committee.

6. Pat Taylor
She had a crush on me when we were at primary school.

7. Mr and Mrs Miller
They're retired and living in Spain now.

8. Eddie Long
He was my boyfriend at school.

9. Billy Baker
His dog used to frighten all the children in the neighbourhood.

Now present your own conversations.

(1) bumped into
ran into

(2) be going
be on my way
be getting on my way/
along
get going (Am.E.)

(3) I have to
I must
I've got to
I'm supposed to

(4) get together soon
keep in touch
stay in touch

(5) Take care.
Take it easy. (Am.E.)

(6) Bye.
Goodbye.

[less formal]
See you.
Cheerio.
Bye-bye.
So long. (Am.E.)

A. Well, it's been really nice seeing you again.
B. Yes, it has. I'm glad we **bumped into**(1) each other.
A. Me, too. You know, I think I should **be going**(2) now.
I have to(3) get this car back to the rental agency by 2:00.
B. Actually, I should be going, too.
A. Let's **get together soon.**(4)
B. Okay. I'll call you.
A. **Take care.**(5)
B. **Bye.**(6)

1. get these packages to the post office before it closes

2. finish my lunch hour a little early today

3. get a few things at the supermarket on my way home

4. be at my piano lesson by 4:00

5. reach Dover by 7:00 tonight

Now present your own conversations.

1.6 Leave taking (2) 'I've really got to go now.'

A. **By the way,**[(1)] **what time is it?**[(2)]
B. It's about 1:30.
A. 1:30?! Already?! I didn't realize it was so late.
B. Neither did I.
A. **I've really got to go now.**[(3)] **I've got to**[(4)] get to my English class.
B. Oh! You'd better hurry! **See you soon.**[(5)]
A. Bye.
B. Bye.

[(1)] By the way,
Incidentally,

[(2)] What time is it?
Have you got the time?
What time do you make it?

[(3)] I've (really) got to go now.
I've (really) got to be going now.
I (really) have to go now.
I'd (really) better go now.
I (really) need to go now.
I (really) should go now.
I (really) must go now.
I have to/I've got to run.
I have to/I've got to get going.

[(4)] I've got to
I have to
I need to
I must

[(5)] (I'll) see you soon/later/ tomorrow/next week/ . . .

1. get to the bank before it closes

2. pick up my daughter at school

3. catch a 3:00 plane

4. be home in time for dinner

5. put my make-up on before the show begins

Now present your own conversations.

9

UNIT 1 SUMMARY

Functions

Meeting and greeting

Hello.
[less formal]
Hi.
[more formal]
How do you do?

(I'm) glad to meet you.
(I'm) pleased to meet you.
(It's) nice to meet you.
(It's) nice meeting you. } (Am.E.)
(I'm) happy to meet you.

How are you?
[less formal]
How are things?
How's it going?
How are you doing? (Am.E.)
  Fine (thank you/thanks).
  All right.
  Okay.
  Not bad.

Introducing

Introducing oneself

My name is _____.
I'm _____.

Introducing others

Let me introduce (you to) _____.
I'd like to introduce (you to) _____.
I'd like you to meet _____.
[less formal]
This is _____.

Leave taking

(You know,) I think I should
{ be going
  be on my way
  be getting on
    my way
  get going (Am.E.) } (now).

I've (really) got to go now.
I've (really) got to be going now.
I (really) have to go now.
I'd (really) better go now.
I (really) need to go now.
I (really) should go now.
I (really) must go now.
I have to/I've got to run.
I have to/I've got to get going.

I should get going, too.

Well, it's been (really) nice seeing you
  again.

Let's get together soon.
Let's keep in touch.
Let's stay in touch.

(I'll) see you soon/later/tomorrow/
  next week/ . . .

I'll call you.

Take care.
Good-bye.
Bye.
Bye-bye.
See you.
Cheerio.
Take it easy. } (Am.E.)
So long.

Surprise/disbelief

1:30?! Already?!

I didn't realize _____.

Asking for and reporting information

Where are you from?
  Japan.
What do you do?
  I'm an *English teacher*.
Which *flat do you live in?*
How long *have you been studying here?*
Who *is your doctor?*
Whose *family do you belong to?*
What kind of *music do you play?*
When *are you due?*

How about you?
What about you?
And you?

Don't you *work in the bank in the
  High Street?*

How is she?
  Fine.
  He/she/they look/s well/okay/fine.

Did _____ say much?

Identifying

My friend *Paul*, my brother *Tom* . . .

She's the one who _____.

Apologizing

I'm sorry.
Excuse me. (Am.E.)

Obligation

Expressing . . .

I have to _____.
I've got to _____.
I'm supposed to _____.
I must _____.

Conversation strategies

Initiating a conversation

I don't think we've met.

Excuse me, but . . .
Pardon me, but . . . (Am.E.)

Don't I know you from somewhere?

Initiating a topic

Guess { who
      what } _____!

You won't believe { who
               what } _____!

Directing/Redirecting a conversation

By the way, . . .
Incidentally, . . .

UNIT 2: GOOD NEWS, BAD NEWS

Passives
Must (deductive)
Present perfect (+ 'just')
Simple past
Going to

2.1 Congratulating 'That's fantastic!'

⁽¹⁾ That's fantastic!
That's great/wonderful/
exciting/marvellous!

⁽²⁾ thrilled
excited
very pleased
ecstatic

⁽³⁾ I'm very happy to hear
that.
I'm very happy for you.
I'm delighted to hear that.

A. I have some good news.
B. Really? What is it?
A. I've just been made assistant manager!
B. Assistant manager?! Really? **That's fantastic!**⁽¹⁾
You must be **thrilled.**⁽²⁾
A. I am.
B. Well, congratulations! **I'm very happy to hear that.**⁽³⁾
A. Thanks.

1. given a big rise

2. offered a place at
university

3. awarded the Nobel Prize
for Physics

4. named 'outstanding
employee of the year'

5. offered a film contract
by a major Hollywood studio

Now present your own
conversations.

12

2.2 Sympathizing 'Oh, that's awful!'

(1) That's awful!
That's a shame/a pity!
What a shame/a pity!
That's terrible!

A. I have some bad news.
B. Oh dear. What is it?
A. My husband's just lost his job.
B. Oh no! Has he really?
A. I'm afraid so.
B. Oh, **that's awful!**(1) You must be very upset.
A. I am.
B. **I'm very sorry to hear that.**(2)

(2) I'm (very) sorry to hear (about) that.
I'm (very/so) sorry.

1. My dog was run over by a car.

2. The factory where I work is going to shut down next month.

3. My son and his wife have decided to get a divorce.

4. I have to stay at home all weekend and take care of my little brother.

5. I was rejected by every medical school I applied to.

'OH, THAT'S AWFUL!'

Now present your own conversations.

2.3 Asking about acquaintances
'Have you heard from your granddaughter lately?'

A. Have you **heard from**[1] your granddaughter lately?
B. As a matter of fact, I have. I **heard from**[1] her just the other day.
A. **How's she doing?**[2]
B. **Fine.**[3] She's getting good marks at school.
A. Is she? That's fantastic!
B. Yes, isn't it.
A. Next time you see her, please **give her my regards.**[4]
B. I certainly will.

A. Have you **run into**[1] your cousin Ralph lately?
B. As a matter of fact, I have. I **ran into**[1] him just the other day.
A. **How is he?**[2]
B. **Not too well.**[5] He had to have four teeth out last week.
A. Really? That's a shame.
B. Yes, isn't it.
A. Next time you see him, please **tell him I'm thinking of him.**[4]
B. OK, I will.

[1] heard from	[2] How's she doing?	[3] Fine.	[4] give her my regards
run into	How is she?	Very well.	tell her/him I'm
talked to	How has she been?		thinking of her/him
seen			remember me to
spoken to			her/him
been in touch	[5] Not too well.		
with	Not very well.		
	Not too good.		

14

1. your parents

2. your neighbours across the road

3. your son

4. your cousins in Coventry

5. George and Irene

6. Janet

7. your friend Elizabeth

8. your grandfather

9. The Chairman

*Parent Teacher Association

Now present your own conversations.

2.4 Passing on news (1) 'Did you hear that school is going to be closed tomorrow?'

(1) You're joking!
I don't/can't believe it!
Oh, come on!
No!
That can't be!
You must be joking!
You're kidding! ⎱
No kidding!   ⎰ (Am.E.)

A. Did you hear (that) school is going to be closed tomorrow?
B. **You're joking!**(1) School isn't really going to be closed tomorrow, is it?
A. Yes, it is.
B. Are you sure?
A. I'm absolutely certain! I heard it on the radio.

1. I saw it in the paper.

2. I heard it on TV.

3. I heard it on the radio.

4. I read it in the morning paper.

5. I heard it on the 7 o'clock news.

Now present your own conversations.

16

2.5 Passing on news (2) 'Have you heard the news?'

A. Have you heard the news?
B. No, what is it?
A. They're going to make the park across the street into a car park.
B. They're going to make the park across the street into a car park?! I don't believe it! **Where did you hear that?**[1]
A. All the neighbours are talking about it.
B. Do you think it's true?
A. I think so, but **I don't know for sure.**[2]
B. Well, personally, I doubt it.

[1] Where did you hear that?
How do you know (that)?
Who told you (that)?

[2] I don't know for sure.
I'm not (completely/ absolutely) certain.
I'm not a hundred percent sure.

1. It's a rumour going around town.

2. I heard it from some people at the supermarket.

3. I overheard some people talking on the bus.

4. It's a rumour going around the office.

5. Some people in my class were talking about it.

Now present your own conversations.

UNIT 2 SUMMARY

Functions

Asking for and reporting information

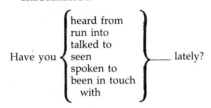

Have you { heard from / run into / talked to / seen / spoken to / been in touch with } _____ lately?

How's _____ doing?
How is _____?
How has _____ been?
  Fine.
  Great.
  Wonderful.
  Not too good.
  Not very well.

Did you hear (that) _____?

Where did you hear that?
How do you know (that)?
Who told you (that)?

I heard it on the radio/on TV/on the news.
I saw/read it in the paper.

School isn't really going to be closed tomorrow, is it?

Sympathizing

That's awful!
That's a shame/a pity!
What a shame/a pity!
That's terrible!

I'm (very) sorry to hear (about) that.
I'm (very/so) sorry.

Certainty/Uncertainty

Inquiring about . . .

Are you sure?

Expressing certainty

I'm absolutely certain!

Expressing uncertainty

I don't know for sure.
I'm not (completely/absolutely) certain.
I'm not a hundred percent sure.
I doubt it.

Congratulating

That's fantastic!
That's great/wonderful/exciting/ marvellous!

Congratulations!

I'm very happy to hear that.
I'm very happy for you.
I'm delighted to hear that.

Deduction

You must be _____.

Surprise/Disbelief

Assistant manager?!

School isn't really going to be closed tomorrow, is it?

They're going to make the park across the street into a car park?!

You're joking!
I don't/can't believe it!
Oh, come on!
No!
That can't be!
You must be joking!

You're kidding! }
No kidding! } (Am.E.)

Conversation strategy

Initiating a topic

I have some good/bad news.

Have you heard the news?

UNIT 3: DESCRIBING AND IDENTIFYING

Adjectives and adjectival phrases
Could/would (requests)
Simple present
The one (with)
Superlatives (the most ... I know)
Past continuous
Simple past

3.1 Describing appearance
'I don't remember what he looks like.'

A. Could you please take these reports over to Charles Jones in Accounts?
B. Certainly. But I'm afraid I don't remember what he looks like.
A. Oh, you can't miss him. He's **about your height**, **rather heavy**, with **dark curly** hair.
B. Okay. I think I'll recognize him.
A. Thanks very much. It's kind of you.

height	*weight*	*hair*		*additional features*
about your height	rather	curly	dark	and (wears) glasses
about average height	very heavy/thin/fat	wavy	light	and (has) a beard/
about _____ feet tall	a little on the plump/	straight	brown	moustache
(very) tall	fat/heavy side	long	black	
(very) short	sort of heavy/thin	short	blond	
a little taller/shorter	(Am.E.)		red	
than you/me			grey	

Complete these conversations using the information above.

1. Could you please take these boxes over to Stella in Shipping?

2. Would you be willing to pick my brother up at the airport?

3. Could you possibly get some chalk from Ms. Crenshaw in the principal's office?

4. Could I possibly ask you to meet my sister at the station?

5. Could I possibly ask you to take another picture of my Uncle Stan?

'WHAT DO THEY LOOK LIKE?'

Now present your own conversations.

3.2 Describing character 'I **wonder what** she's **like**.'

A. Our new English teacher starts today. I wonder what she's like. **Have you heard anything**[1] about her?
B. Yes. **People say**[2] she's very intelligent.
A. Hmm. **What else have you heard?**[3]
B. Well, they also say she's very patient.
A. Really? That's interesting.

[1] Have you heard anything
    Do you know anything

[2] People say
    They say
    People/They tell me
    Everybody says
    Everybody tells me
    I've heard
    I'm told

[3] What else have you heard?
    Have you heard anything else?
    Do you know anything else?

1. the new boss
   bright
   strict

2. the new caretaker
   friendly
   helpful

3. the new student in our class
   nice
   outgoing

4. the new energy minister
   articulate
   clever

5. the new foreman
   unfriendly
   short-tempered

Now present your own conversations.

3.3 Describing jobs 'What do you do?'

(1) I don't know where to
    begin.
    I don't know where to
    start.
    I don't know what to say.

(2) What do you want to
    know?
    What would you like to
    know?
    What can I tell you?

(3) exciting
    interesting
    challenging
    difficult
    important
    creative
    .
    .
    .

A. So, tell me something about yourself.
B. Well, er, ... **I don't know where to begin.**(1)
   What do you want to know?(2)
A. Well, let's see ... What do you do?
B. I'm a civil engineer.
A. That sounds interesting. Do you enjoy your work?
B. Yes. I like it a lot.
A. Tell me, what exactly do you do?
B. Well, I design roads and bridges.
A. Oh. That sounds like a very **exciting**(3) job.
B. It is.

1. I'm a barrister.
I defend people accused of crimes.

2. I'm a speech writer.
I write speeches for politicians.

3. I'm an administrative assistant.
I handle all the business communication
for the director of my company.

4. I'm an ambulance driver.
I drive an ambulance and answer 999 calls.

5. I'm an estate agent.
I help people who want to buy or sell
a house.

6. I'm an anthropologist.
I study people from different cultures
all over the world.

7. I'm a computer programmer.
I design computer programs for
business and industry.

8. I'm a meteorologist.
I give the weather forecasts on TV.

9. I'm a stunt performer.
I jump out of blazing houses or fall off
horses in films.

'WHAT DO YOU DO?'

Now present your own conversations.

3.4 Identifying objects 'Which one?'

(1) You should wear _____.
Why don't you wear _____?
How about wearing _____?

The children gave you a *blue* tie *with grey and yellow stripes.*

A. **You should wear**(1) your new tie with that jacket.
B. Which one?
A. The one the children gave you.
B. Hmm. Which one is that?
A. You remember. It's the *blue* one *with grey and yellow stripes.*
B. Oh, that one. I know where it is. I'll get it.

1. I gave you a *purple* bathing suit *with yellow spots.*

2. Aunt Margaret sent you a *woollen* sweater *made in Scotland.*

3. The people at the office gave you a *red* scarf *made of silk.*

4. Uncle Harry gave us a *pocket-sized* camera *in a brown leather case.*

5. Granny sent you a *pretty* doll *that cries when you pull the string.*

Now present your own conversations.

3.5 Describing places 'Can you tell me what it's like there?'

A. Have you by any chance ever been to Hong Kong?
B. Yes, I have. Why?
A. I'm going there with my family for a holiday next month. Can you tell me what it's like there?
B. Well, it's a very *exciting* place. **As a matter of fact,**[1] it's probably one of the *most exciting* places I know.
A. Really? That's good to hear. **Can you tell me anything else?**[2]
B. Well ... what else would you like to know?
A. How about the weather ... and the people?
B. The weather at this time of year is usually *cool*, and **in my opinion,**[3] the people there are very *interesting*.
A. It sounds a wonderful place.
B. It is. I'm sure you'll have a good time there.

[1] As a matter of fact,
In fact,

[2] Can you tell me anything else?
Can you tell me anything more?
What else can you tell me?

[3] in my opinion,
if you ask me,
as far as I'm concerned,

1. dynamic
warm
nice

2. beautiful
pleasant
formal

3. dramatic
hot
hospitable

4. charming
wet
helpful

5. lively
comfortable
friendly

'WHAT'S IT LIKE THERE?'

Now present your own conversations

3.6 INTERCHANGE: Describing a sequence of events
What happened?

A. What happened?
B. Well, I was lying on the beach listening to the radio, when suddenly I heard someone shouting for help.
A. So what did you do?
B. I jumped up, looked out to sea, and saw a little boy waving his arms in the air.
A. **What did you do next?**[1]
B. I took off my shirt and my watch and jumped into the water.
A. **And THEN what did you do?**[1]
B. I swam out to the little boy, held him so his head stayed above water and brought him back to shore.
A. Well, that sounds like it was quite an experience!
B. It certainly was!

A. What happened?
B. Well, I was _____ing, when suddenly _____.
A. So what did you do?
B. _____.
A. **What did you do next?**[1]
B. _____.
A. **And THEN what did you do?**[1]
B. _____.
A. Well, that sounds like it was quite an experience!
B. It certainly was!

---

[1] What did you do next?   And then what did you do?
    What did you do after that?   What was the next thing you did?

1.

2.

You're telling somebody about something that happened. Create an original conversation using the model dialogue on p. 26 as a guide. Feel free to adapt and expand the model any way you wish.

UNIT 3 SUMMARY

Functions

Asking for and reporting information

Which one is that?

Have you by any chance ever _____ed?

Can you tell me what it's like?

What happened?

Have you heard anything about _____?
Do you know anything about _____?

People say . . .
They say . . .
People/They tell me . . .
Everybody says . . .
Everybody tells me . . .
I've heard . . .
I'm told . . .

Tell me something about yourself.

What do you want to know?
What would you like to know?
What can I tell you?

Asking for and reporting additional information

What else have you heard?
Have you heard anything else?
Do you know anything else?

Can you tell me anything else?
Can you tell me anything more?
What else can you tell me?

What did you do next?
What did you do after that?
And then what did you do?
What was the next thing you did?

What else would you like to know?

As a matter of fact, . . .
In fact, . . .

Describing

He's about your height, rather heavy, with dark curly hair.

He's/She's very _____.

It's the _____ one with the _____.

It's a (very) _____ _____.

It's one of the _____est _____s I know.

Identifying

The one *the children gave you.*

Advice/Suggestions

Offering . . .

You should _____.
Why don't you _____?
How about _____ing?

Requests

Direct, more polite

Could you please _____?
Could you possibly _____?
Could I possibly ask you to _____?
Would you be willing to _____?

Remembering/Forgetting

You remember.

Oh, that one.

Conversation strategies

Focusing attention

As a matter of fact, . . .
In fact, . . .

In my opinion, . . .
If you ask me, . . .
As far as I'm concerned, . . .

Hesitating

Well, er, . . .

I don't know where to begin.
I don't know where to start.
I don't know what to say.

Well, let's see . . .

SCENES AND IMPROVISATIONS
Units 1–3

Who do you think these people are?
What do you think they're talking about?
Create conversations based on these scenes and act them out.

1.

2.

3.

4.

5.

6.

7.

8.

UNIT 4: SATISFACTION AND DISSATISFACTION

Adjectives (too ..., ... enough, as ... as)
Comparatives
Superlatives (one of the most ...)
Present continuous (− 'always'/'constantly')

4.1 Complimenting (1) 'That was a very good performance.'

(1) a very good
quite a

[less formal]
some (Am.E.)

(2) Yes.
Very much.
Absolutely. (Am.E.)

(3) excellent
wonderful
terrific
magnificent
fabulous
superb

(4) Thanks/Thank you (for saying so).
It's nice/kind of you to say so/that.

A. That was **a very good**(1) performance!
B. Did you really like it?
A. **Yes.**(2) I thought it was **excellent.**(3)
B. **Thanks for saying so.**(4)

1. dinner

2. lecture

3. presentation

4. party

5. speech

Now present your own conversations.

4.2 Complimenting (2) 'I really like your flat.'

A. I **really like**[1] your flat. It's **very**[2] spacious.
B. **Oh, go on!**[3] You're just saying that!
A. No. **I mean it!**[4] It's one of the most spacious flats I've ever seen.
B. Well, thanks for saying so. I'm glad you like it.

---

[1] (really)/(do) like
     love

[2] very
     so

[3] Oh, go on!
     Oh, come on!
     Oh!

[4] I mean it!
     I'm (really/quite) serious.
     I'm being perfectly honest.

1. tie
attractive

2. dress
pretty

3. painting
interesting

4. blouse
colourful

5. haircut
nice

'I REALLY LIKE YOUR....'

Now present your own conversations.

(1) How do you like
What do you think of

(2) fine
very nice
perfect

(3) satisfied
happy
pleased

(4) Very.
Yes.

(5) just what I
had in mind/
wanted/was
looking for

A. **How do you like**(1) the bicycle?
B. It's **fine.**(2)
A. It isn't too heavy?
B. No, not at all.
A. Is it large enough?
B. Oh, yes. I wouldn't want it any larger.
A. So you're **satisfied**(3) with it?
B. **Very.**(4) It's **just what I had in mind!**(5)

1. mattress
short
firm

2. tennis racket
big
light

3. wedding dress
plain
fancy

4. trousers
tight
long

5. gloves
bulky
warm

Now present your own
conversations.

4.4 Expressing dissatisfaction (1)
'I'd just like a refund, please.'

A. I'd like to return this hat.
B. **What seems to be the problem with it?**[1]
A. It's too old-fashioned.
B. Would you like to exchange it for one that's more modern?
A. **I don't think so.**[2] I'd just like a refund, please.
B. I'm sorry. We don't give refunds. **However,**[3] we'll be happy to give you a credit note.
A. No refunds?
B. I'm afraid not.
A. Oh. Thanks anyway.

[1] What seems to be the problem (with it)?
What seems to be the matter (with it)?
What's the problem/the matter/wrong (with it)?

[2] I don't think so.
Not really.
No, thank you.

[3] However,
But

1. coat
long
short

2. sports shirt
flashy
conservative

3. DIY book
complicated
simple

4. video game
easy
challenging

5. parrot
talkative
quiet

'I'D JUST LIKE A REFUND, PLEASE.'

Now present your own conversations.

35

(1) to tell (you) the truth,
honestly,
to be honest (with you),

(2) I was (a little) disappointed.
I wasn't very pleased with
it.
I didn't think much of it.
It was (a little) disappointing.

(3) Why?
How come? (Am.E.)

(4) expected it to be
thought it would be
hoped it would be

How did you like the play?
B. Well, **to tell the truth**(1) **I was a little disappointed.**(2)
A. **Why?**(3)
B. It wasn't as funny as I thought it would be.
I really **expected it to be**(4) a lot funnier.
A. That's a pity.

1. your holiday
relaxing

2. the match
exciting

3. the steak
juicy

4. your date with Ted last night
enjoyable

5. English class today
good

Now present your own
conversations.

4.6 Expressing dissatisfaction (3)
'I'm very **annoyed** with my landlord,'

A. I'm very **annoyed with**(1) my landlord.
B. Why?
A. **He's always**(2) forgetting to mend things.
B. Have you spoken to him about it?
A. Well, no, I haven't.
B. I don't understand. If it **bothers**(3) you so much, why don't you **mention it to him?**(4)
A. I suppose I should. But I don't like complaining.

(1) annoyed with
    upset with

    [stronger]
    angry with
    furious with
    mad at (Am.E.)

(2) He's always
    He's constantly
    He keeps on

(3) bothers
    annoys
    upsets

(4) mention it to him
    talk to him about it
    discuss it with him
    bring up the subject
        with him

1. My secretary is always making spelling mistakes.

2. My neighbours are always playing their stereo after midnight.

3. My teacher is always giving us homework over the weekend.

4. My roommate is always snoring at night.

5. My parents are always treating me like a baby.

'I'M VERY ANNOYED...'

Now present your own conversations.

4.7 INTERCHANGE: Discussing likes and dislikes
'Would you like to do something this weekend?'

A. Would you like to do something this weekend?
B. Okay. What would you like to do?
A. Well, how about seeing a film?
B. That sounds good. Did you have any particular film in mind?
A. Well, they say that 'A man and his horse' is very good. It's on at the Curzon.
B. 'A man and his horse'? That's a **western,**[1] isn't it?
A. I think so.
B. Well, to tell the truth, **I don't like westerns**[1] **very much.**[2]
A. Oh. Well, is there any particular film you'd like to see?
B. How about 'The Return of the Monster'? It's on at the ABC, and I hear it's excellent.
A. 'Return of the Monster'? Hmm. Isn't that a **science fiction film?**
B. Yes. Don't you like **science fiction films?**[1]
A. No, not really. Maybe we shouldn't see a film. Maybe we should do something else.
B. Okay. Would you be interested in doing something outdoors?
A. Yes. Any suggestions?
B. Well, we could go skating.
A. Oh. I'm afraid **I don't really enjoy**[2] skating. How about going hiking?
B. Well, to tell the truth, I've gone hiking several times in the past few weeks.
A. Really? Then you must be pretty **tired of**[3] hiking.
B. I am. Let's do something else.
A. Why don't we just have dinner together somewhere this Saturday?
B. Good idea. Where would you like to go?
A. Well, one of my favourite places to eat is 'The Captain's Table'.
B. Hmm. 'The Captain's Table'? What kind of food do they serve there?
A. **Seafood.**[4] But if you don't like **seafood,**[4] we can go somewhere else.
B. No. On the contrary, I LOVE **seafood!**[4]
A. You do?! Great!
B. Then **it's settled.**[5] 'The Captain's Table' for dinner on Saturday. What time?
A. How about 7 o'clock?
B. Is 8 okay?
A. Fine.

38

(1)
western	adventure film	foreign film
comedy	science fiction film	cartoon
mystery	documentary	tear-jerker
drama	children's film	pornographic film
	(movie: Am.E.)	

(2)
I don't (really) like/enjoy
_____ very much.
I don't (particularly) care
for _____.
I'm not (really) keen on
_____.
[stronger]
I hate _____.

(3)
tired of
sick of
sick and tired of

(4)
seafood
steak and potatoes
pizza
fried chicken
vegetarian food
Greek food
Chinese food

(5)
It's settled.
That's settled.
We're agreed.

A. Would you like to do something this weekend?
B. Okay. What would you like to do?
A. Well, how about seeing a film?
B. That sounds good. Did you have any particular film in mind?
A. Well, they say that '_____' is very good. It's on at the _____.
B. '_____'? That's a _____,(1) isn't it?
A. I think so.
B. Well, to tell the truth, **I don't like** _____s(1) **very much.**(2)
A. Oh. Well, is there any particular film you'd like to see?
B. How about '_____'? It's on at the _____, and I hear it's excellent.
A. '_____'? Hmm. Isn't that a _____?(1)
B. Yes. Don't you like _____s?(1)
A. No, not really. Maybe we shouldn't see a film. Maybe we should do something else.
B. Okay. Would you be interested in doing something outdoors?
A. Yes. Any suggestions?
B. Well, we could go _____ing.
A. Oh. I'm afraid **I don't really enjoy**(2) _____ing. How about going _____ing?
B. Well, to tell the truth, I've gone _____ing several times in the past few weeks.
A. Really? Then you must be pretty **tired of**(3) _____ing.
B. I am. Let's do something else.
A. Why don't we just have dinner together somewhere this Saturday?
B. Good idea. Where would you like to go?
A. Well, one of my favourite places to eat is '_____'.
B. Hmm. '_____'? What kind of food do they serve there?
A. _____.(4) But if you don't like _____,(4) we can go somewhere else.
B. No. On the contrary, I LOVE _____!(4)
A. You do?! Great!
B. Then **it's settled.**(5) '_____' for dinner on Saturday. What time?
A. How about _____ o'clock?
B. Is _____ okay?
A. Fine.

Create an original conversation using the model dialogue above as a guide. In your conversation, use the names of films, cinemas, and restaurants where you live, and refer to outdoor activities you enjoy doing at the weekend. Feel free to adapt and expand the model in any way you wish.

UNIT 4 SUMMARY

Functions

Satisfaction/Dissatisfaction

Enquiring about . . .

How do you like _____?
What do you think of _____?

How did you like _____?

Did you (really) like it?

Are you $\begin{cases} \text{satisfied} \\ \text{happy} \\ \text{pleased} \end{cases}$ with it?

Is it _____ enough?

What seems to be the problem (with it)?
What seems to be the matter (with it)?
What's the problem/the matter/wrong (with it)?

Expressing satisfaction

It's $\begin{cases} \text{fine.} \\ \text{very nice.} \\ \text{perfect.} \end{cases}$

It's just what I $\begin{cases} \text{had in mind.} \\ \text{wanted.} \\ \text{was looking for.} \end{cases}$

I wouldn't want it any _____er.

Expressing dissatisfaction

It's too _____.

I really $\begin{cases} \text{expected it to be} \\ \text{thought it would be} \\ \text{hoped it would be} \end{cases}$ _____er.

It wasn't as _____ as I thought it would be.

Gratitude

Expressing . . .

Thanks/Thank you (for saying so).
It's nice of you to say so/that.

Persuading/Insisting

I mean it!
I'm (really/quite) serious.
I'm being perfectly honest.

Likes/Dislikes

Enquiring about . . .

How do you like _____?
What do you think of _____?

How did you like _____?

Did you like _____?

Don't you like _____?

Expressing likes

I like _____.
I love _____.

Expressing dislikes

I don't (really) like/enjoy _____ very much.
I don't (particularly) care for _____.
I'm not (really) keen on _____.
[stronger]
I hate _____.

Complimenting

Expressing compliments

That was $\begin{cases} \text{a very good} \\ \text{quite a} \\ \text{[less formal]} \\ \text{some (Am.E.)} \end{cases}$ _____!

I thought it was $\begin{cases} \text{excellent.} \\ \text{wonderful.} \\ \text{terrific.} \\ \text{magnificent.} \\ \text{fabulous.} \\ \text{superb.} \end{cases}$

I (really) like _____.
I love _____.

It's very _____.
It's so _____.

It's one of the _____est _____s I've ever _____ed.

Responding to compliments

Thanks/Thank you (for saying so).
It's nice/kind of you to say so/that.
I'm glad you like it.

Oh, go on!
Oh, come on!
Oh!

You're just saying that.

Disappointment

I was (a little) disappointed.
I wasn't very pleased with it.
I didn't think much of it.
It was (a little) disappointing.

Complaining

It's too _____.

I was (a little) disappointed.
I wasn't very pleased with it.
It was (a little) disappointing.

I'm $\begin{cases} \text{annoyed with} \\ \text{upset with} \\ \text{[stronger]} \\ \text{angry with} \\ \text{furious with} \\ \text{mad at (Am.E.)} \end{cases}$ _____.

He's always
He's constantly _____ing.
He keeps on

I'm tired of _____(ing).
I'm sick of _____(ing).
I'm sick and tired of _____(ing).

Advice/Suggestions

Offering . . .

How about _____?
How about _____ing?
Would you be interested in _____?
We could _____.
Why don't we _____?
Let's _____.

Why don't you _____?

Have you _____ed?

Maybe we should _____.
Maybe we shouldn't _____.

They say that _____ is very good.
One of my favourite _____s is _____.

Is _____ okay?

40

UNIT 5: PREFERENCES, DISAGREEMENT AND NEUTRALITY

I'd like/I'd prefer
Would you like to ...?
Gerunds (feel like _____ing)
Present perfect continuous
I'd rather (+ simple present)

5.1 Expressing preferences (1) **'I'd prefer** a baked potato.'

(1) I'd like
I'll have
I want

(2) prefer
rather have
like

a steak
rare
a baked potato
a cup of coffee

A. Can I help you?
B. Yes, **I'd like**(1) a steak.
A. How would you like it?
B. Rare.
A. Okay. And would you **prefer**(2) a baked potato or rice with it?
B. I'd **prefer**(2) a baked potato.
A. Anything to drink?
B. A cup of coffee, please.
A. Okay. That's a rare steak with a baked potato and a cup of coffee.

a hamburger
well-done
chips
a Coke

1. chips or boiled potatoes?

the chicken
grilled
a salad
a glass of white
white

2. a salad or a vegetable?

an egg
scrambled
toast
a glass of milk

3. toast or a roll?

a cheese sandwich
grilled
potato salad
a glass of lemonade

4. potato salad or coleslaw?

the fish
poached
rice
a glass of milk

5. rice or mashed potatoes?

'I'D PREFER...'

Now present your own conversations.

5.2 Expressing preferences (2) 'I'd much rather see a film.'

(1) Would you like to
     Would you prefer to
     Would you rather

(2) I'd prefer to
     I'd rather
     I'd like to

(3) I (really) don't feel like
     _____ing.
     I'm not (really) in the
     mood for _____ing.
     I'd (really) prefer not to
     _____.

A. **Would you like to**(1) stay at home or see a film?
B. I think **I'd prefer to**(2) stay at home. How about you?
A. Well, to be honest, **I really don't feel like**(3) staying at home. I'd much rather see a film. Is that okay with you?
B. Yes. We haven't seen a film for a long time anyway.

1. eat at home or in a restaurant?

2. swim in the sea or in the pool?

3. walk home or take a taxi?

4. watch the match on TV or go to the stadium?

5. put Rover in the boarding kennels or take him on holiday with us?

'I'D MUCH RATHER...'

Now present your own conversations.

43

5.3 Talking about a disagreement 'Is anything wrong?'

(1) You've seemed troubled
You've seemed upset
You've seemed preoccupied
You haven't been yourself

(2) wrong
the matter
on your mind

(3) settle it
resolve it
find a solution

A. **You've seemed troubled**(1) for the past few days. Is anything **wrong?**(2)
B. Well, to tell the truth, I've been having a disagreement with my boss.
A. Oh? What's it all about?
B. Well, to cut a long story short, my boss wants me to work on the night shift, but I'd rather stay on the day shift.
A. Does he feel strongly about your working on the night shift?
B. Yes, he does. And I feel just as strongly about staying on the day shift.
A. Well, it sounds like a serious disagreement. I hope you can **settle it**(3) soon.
B. So do I.

1. my mother

2. my wife

3. my parents

4. my business partner

5. my family

6. my husband

7. the people in my parish

8. my economic adviser

9. some members of my trade union

Now present your own conversations.

5.4 Expressing neutrality (1) 'It makes no difference.'

(1) have any strong feelings about it
have any feelings about it one way or another
care one way or another
have a preference/any preferences

(2) It makes no difference (to me).
It doesn't make any difference (to me).
It doesn't matter (to me).
It's all the same to me.
I don't mind.
I don't feel strongly about it (one way or the other).

A. When do you want to leave?
B. Oh. I don't know. Whenever you'd like to leave is fine with me.
A. You don't **have any strong feelings about it?**(1)
B. No, not really. **It makes no difference.**(2)

1. Who would you like to invite to the party?

2. What would you like to do this weekend?

3. Which film would you rather see?

4. How would you like me to cut your hair?

5. Where do you want us to put the couch?

Now present your own conversations.

5.5 Expressing neutrality (2) 'It's entirely up to you.'

A. **Would you mind**[1] if I went home early?
B. No, not at all.
A. Are you sure? I mean if you'd rather I didn't I won't.
B. No. Honestly. It doesn't matter to me whether you go home early or not. **It's entirely up to you.**[2]

[1] Would you mind
Would it bother you
Would it disturb you

[2] It's (entirely) up to you.
It's (entirely) your decision.
It's for you to decide.

1. smoke

2. invite my boss for dinner

3. drop something off at the post office

4. make the bed now

5. have a date with someone else

'IT'S ENTIRELY UP TO YOU.'

Now present your own conversations.

5.6 INTERCHANGE: Expressing preferences (3)
'I'd like the fruit juice.'

A. Welcome to 'The International Gourmet'. Would you like to see the menu, or would you care to order today's set dinner?

B. What's the main dish?

A. Leg of lamb ... and I can highly recommend it.

B. Well ... Let me see ... Okay. I think I'll have the set dinner.

A. All right. Now, as a starter you have a choice of fruit juice or tomato juice.

B. Hmm. I think I'd like the fruit juice.

A. All right. And the soups we're offering today are split pea or French onion.

B. Split pea or French onion? Hmm. That's a difficult choice. I think I'd rather have the split pea.

A. And what kind of dressing would you like on your salad?

B. What do you have?

A. Well, let's see. We have Italian, French and Russian.

B. I'd prefer Italian.

A. Italian. Fine. Now, with your leg of lamb, you can have your choice of two vegetables. Today we're featuring brown rice, baked potato, French beans in a cream sauce, and ... Hmm ... Let me see if I can remember them all ... Oh, yes ... And we also have peas, spinach or mushrooms.

B. That's quite a selection! Let's see ... uh ... hmmm. I'll have French beans and a baked potato.

A. Right. I think that's it. Oh! I almost forgot. What would you like to drink with your meal?

B. I'll have a glass of red wine.

A. Good. I'll put your order in at once, and I'll be back in a moment with some rolls and butter.

B. Thank you.

A. Welcome to '_____'. Would you like to see the menu, or would you care to order today's set dinner?
B. What's the main dish?
A. _____ ... and I can highly recommend it.
B. Well ... Let me see ... Okay. I think I'll have the set dinner.
A. All right. Now, as a starter you have a choice of _____ or _____.
B. Hmm. I think I'd like the _____.
A. All right. And the soups we're offering are _____ or _____.
B. _____ or _____? Hmm. That's a difficult choice. I think I'd rather have the _____.
A. And what kind of dressing would you like on your salad?
B. What do you have?
A. Well, let's see. We have _____, _____ and _____.
B. I'd prefer _____.
A. _____. Fine. Now, with your _____, you can have your choice of two vegetables. Today we're featuring _____, _____, _____, and ... Hmm ... Let me see if I can remember them all ... Oh, yes ... And we also have _____.
B. That's quite a selection! Let's see ... uh ... hmmm. I'll have _____ and _____.
A. Right. I think that's it. Oh! I almost forgot. What would you like to drink with your meal?
B. I'll have _____.
A. Good. I'll put your order in at once, and I'll be back in a moment with some rolls and butter.
B. Thank you.

You're a waiter or waitress in a restaurant. Give your restaurant a name, design a 'main dish' for your 'set dinner', and then create an original conversation using the model dialogue above as a guide. Feel free to adapt and expand the model in any way you wish.

(Use the 'memo' below to design your 'main dish' for your 'set dinner'.)

MEMO TO ALL WAITERS AND WAITRESSES

Please let your customers know that today's set dinner is as follows:

Main dish: _____

Starters: _____   Soups: _____

_____   _____

Salad Dressings: Vegetables:

_____   _____ _____

_____   _____ _____

_____   _____

UNIT 5 SUMMARY

Functions

Preference

Enquiring about . . .

Would you {
  prefer _____?
  rather have _____?
  like _____?
}

Would you like to
Would you prefer to
Would you rather
Would you care to
} _____ (or _____)?

How would you like it?

Do you have any strong feelings about it?
Do you have any feelings about it one way or another?
Do you care one way or another?
Do you have a preference/any preferences?

Expressing . . .

I'd prefer _____.
I'd rather have _____.
I'd like _____.

I'd prefer to _____.
I'd rather _____.
I'd like to _____.
I'd much rather _____.

I'd prefer not to _____.

I feel strongly about _____ing.

If you'd rather I didn't _____, I won't.

Want/Desire

Enquiring about . . .

When do you want to _____?
Who would you like to _____?
What would you like to do?
How would you like me to _____?
Which _____ would you rather _____?
Where do you want _____ to _____?

Expressing . . .

I'd like _____.
I'll have _____.
I want _____.

I (really) don't feel like _____ing.
I'm not (really) in the mood for _____ing.
I'd (really) prefer not to _____.

_____ wants me to _____.

Requests

Direct, more polite

Would you mind
Would it bother you
Would it disturb you
} if I _____ed?

Neutrality

Whenever _____ is fine with me.
(Whoever . . . Whatever . . .
  However . . . Whichever . . .
  Wherever . . .)

It makes no difference (to me).
It doesn't matter (to me).
It's all the same to me.
I don't mind.
I don't feel strongly about it (one way or the other).

It doesn't matter to me whether you _____ or not.

It's (entirely) up to you.
It's (entirely) your decision.
It's for you to decide.

Conversation strategy

Hesitating

Well . . .
Let me see . . .
Let's see . . .
Hmm . . .
Okay . . .
Er . . .
I think . . .

UNIT 6: PROMISES

6.1 *Making promises* (1)
'**You can rely on me.**'

6.2 *Making promises* (2)
'**I won't let you down.**'

6.3 *False promises* (1)
'That salesman's **really let me down.**'

6.4 *False promises* (2)
'**I'm afraid I wasn't able to do it.**'

Summary

Future (will)
Going to
Supposed to
Able to
Simple past with emphatic 'did'

6.1 Making promises (1) 'You can rely on me.'

(1) rely on
depend on
count on

(2) I promise I'll
I promise to

A. Can I **rely on**(1) you to turn off the lights when you leave?
B. Yes. **I promise I'll**(2) turn them off.
A. You won't forget? It's really important.
B. Don't worry. You can **rely on**(1) me.

1. pick up the drinks for the party tonight

2. bring back my typewriter tomorrow

3. drop my suit off at the cleaner's on your way to college

4. put away your toys before our guests arrive

5. clean up the kitchen before the environmental health officer gets here

Now present your own conversations.

6.2 Making promises (2) 'I won't let you down.'

A. Will the car be ready by five?
B. Yes, it will.
A. Really? Can I **depend on**(1) that?
B. **Of course!**(2) **I promise**(3) it'll be ready by five.
A. Okay. Now remember, I'm **counting**(4) on you.
B. Don't worry! I won't **let you down.**(5)

(1) depend on
count on
rely on
be sure of

(2) Of course!
Absolutely!
Definitely!

(3) I promise (you)
I guarantee
I (can) assure you
I give you my word
You can be sure

(4) counting
depending
relying

(5) let you down
disappoint you

1. Will you write to me often?

2. Will we get to the airport in time for my 3:00 flight?

3. Will there be enough food for all our customers tonight?

4. Will this extraction be painless?

5. Will you behave yourself for the baby-sitter tonight?

Now present your own conversations.

6.3 Falbe promises (1) 'That salesman's **really let me down.'**

A. That salesman's really let me down. I'm very **annoyed with**[1] him.
B. Oh dear! Why is that?
A. He guaranteed that this watch was waterproof, but it isn't!
B. **That's a shame.**[2] Are you going to talk to him about it? After all, he DID give you his word.
A. **Maybe I should.**[3]

A. My next-door neighbour's really let me down. I'm very **annoyed with**[1] her.
B. Oh dear? Why is that?
A. She gave me her word she'd keep her dog off my lawn, but she hasn't!
B. **That's a shame.**[2] Are you going to talk to her about it? After all, she DID give you her word.
A. **Maybe I should.**[3]

[1] annoyed with disappointed with disappointed in	[2] That's/What a shame. That's a pity. That's too bad. (Am.E.)	[3] Maybe/Perhaps I should. I suppose I will. I guess I will. (Am.E.)

1. my upstairs neighbour

2. my landlord

3. my daughter

4. my boss

5. my employees

6. the photographer

7. my agent in Hollywood

Now present your own conversations.

(1) annoyed
disappointed
upset

(2) What makes you say that?
Why do you say that?
Why?
How come? (Am.E.)

(3) I was supposed to
I said I would
I had promised to
I had promised you I
    would

(4) I wasn't able to
I couldn't

(5) The truth is (that)
The fact of the matter is
    that

(6) you were counting/
    depending on me to
    _____

you were counting/
    depending on my
    _____ing

you had expected me
    to _____

A. You're going to be very **annoyed**(1) with me.
B. **What makes you say that?**(2)
A. Well, remember **I was supposed to**(3) save you a seat?
B. Yes . . .?
A. Well, . . . I'm afraid **I wasn't able to**(4) do it.
B. Oh? Why not?
A. **The truth is,**(5) I tried to but the usherette wouldn't let me.
B. Don't worry about it.
A. I am sorry. After all, **you were counting on me to**(6) save it.
B. Don't worry about it. These things happen.
A. You aren't annoyed?
B. No, it's okay.

1. fix your doorbell

2. pick up your dress at the cleaner's

3. do the shopping on the way home

4. clean the flat this week

5. get these copied for you

6. get at least a B in my biology test

7. finish your sweater in time for your birthday

8. return your library book

9. get you reservations at the Plaza Hotel

Now present your own conversations.

UNIT 6 SUMMARY

Functions

Promising

Asking for a promise

Can I { rely on / depend on / count on } you to _____?

Can I { depend on / count on / rely on / be sure of } that?

Making a promise

Promise.
I promise I'll _____.
I promise to _____.

I promise (you) _____.
I guarantee _____.
I can assure you _____.
I give you my word _____.
You can be sure _____.

Absolutely.
Definitely.
Of course.

You can { rely on / depend on / count on } me.

I won't let you down.
I won't disappoint you.

Disappointment

I'm (very) disappointed with/in _____.

I'm very annoyed with _____.

Sympathizing

That's a/What a shame.
That's a pity.
That's too bad. (Am.E.)

Denying/Admitting

Admitting

I'm afraid _____.

The truth is (that) _____.
The fact of the matter is (that) _____.

Obligation

Expressing . . .

I was supposed to _____.
I said I would _____.
I had promised to _____.
I had promised you I would _____.

You were counting/depending on me to _____.
You were counting/depending on my _____ing.
You had expected me to _____.

Ability/Inability

Expressing inability

I wasn't able to _____.
I couldn't _____.

Asking for and reporting information

What makes you say that?
Why do you say that?
Why?
How come? (Am.E.)

Conversation strategy

Hesitating

Well, . . .

SCENES AND IMPROVISATIONS
Units 4–6

Who do you think these people are?
What do you think they're talking about?
Create conversations based on these scenes and act them out.

1.

2.

3.

4.

5.

6.

7.

8.

UNIT 7: DECISIONS, PLANS AND INTENTIONS

7.1 *Making a decision* (1)
'I've made a decision.'

7.2 *Making plans* (1)
'I'll probably stay at home and read a book.'

7.3 *Making a decision* (2)
'I haven't made up my mind yet.'

7.4 *Making plans* (2)
'I was planning to do it later.'

7.5 *Expectations*
'As far as I know, he's going to arrive at 2:30.'

7.6 *Unfulfilled intentions*
'I forgot all about it.'

7.7 *Changing plans*
'I won't be able to go bowling with you.'

7.8 *Interchange: Discussing past plans and decisions*
'I changed my mind.'

Summary

Going to
Present continuous expressing future
Gerunds
Present perfect continuous
Present perfect (+ 'yet')
Would you mind _____?
Passives
Past continuous

7.1 Making a decision (1) 'I've made a decision.'

(1) I'm going to
I'm planning to
I plan to
I intend to
I've decided to

(2) Really?
Good heavens!
My word!
Gee!
Boy! } (Am.E.)
Wow!

(3) I've thought about it for a
long time
I've given it a lot of
thought
I've given it a lot of
(serious) consideration

A. You know, ... I've made a decision.
B. What?
A. **I'm going to**(1) join the army.
B. **Really?**(2) Join the army! That's a big decision!
A. I know it is. But **I've thought about it for a long time**(3) and decided it's time to do it.
B. Well, good luck!

1. get married

2. give up smoking

3. sell my house

4. leave my job

5. emigrate

'I'VE MADE A DECISION.'

Now present your own conversations.

7.2 Making plans (1)
'I'll **probably** stay at home and read a book.'

A. Hello! It's me!
B. Oh, hi! How are you?
A. Fine. Tell me, what are you doing this afternoon?
B. **I'm not sure.**[1] **I'll probably**[2] stay at home and read a book. How about you?
A. Well, I'm planning to go fishing. **Would you like to join me?**[3]
B. Yes, **I'd like to.**[4] Going fishing sounds a lot more **exciting**[5] than staying at home and reading a book.
A. Good! I'll pick you up at around one o'clock.
B. See you then.

[1] I'm not sure.
     I'm not certain.
     I don't know yet.

[2] probably
     most likely

[3] Would you like to join me?
     Do you want to join me?
     Would you be interested in joining me?

[4] I'd like to.
     I'd love to.
     I'd like that.
     I'd be happy to. (Am.E.)

[5] exciting
     enjoyable
     interesting
     fun

1. work in the garden
   play tennis

2. work on my car
   go swimming

3. do some jobs around the house
   see the exhibition of Chinese art

4. work on my essay
   see a film

5. catch up on some work at the office
   play a few holes of golf

'I'LL PROBABLY...'

Now present your own conversations.

7.3 Making a decision (2) 'I haven't made up my mind yet.'

(1) I've been thinking of
I'm thinking of
I've been thinking about
I'm thinking about

(2) I thought I might
I thought I'd
I might
I may

A. Have you decided who you're going to ask to the dance?
B. No. I haven't made up my mind yet. **I've been thinking of**(1) asking Susan, but **I** also **thought I might**(2) ask Elizabeth.
A. Sounds like a difficult decision. I'll be curious to know what you decide.
B. I'll let you know.
A. Promise?
B. Promise.

1. Chemistry
Music

2. to Spain
to Malta

3. right away
when business gets better

4. on our next date
in a long letter

5. a racer
a mountain bike

Now present your own conversations.

7.4 Making plans (2) 'I was planning to do it later.'

A. Have you done Room 407 yet?
B. No, I haven't. **I was planning to**[1] do it **later.**[2]
A. Would you mind doing it soon?
B. No, not at all. I'll do it **right away.**[3]

[1]
I was planning to
I was going to
I intended to
I thought I would

[2]
later
in a little while

[3]
right away
right now
as soon as I can
at the first chance I get

1. write the monthly report

2. copy my memo

3. distribute the mail

4. make my hotel reservations

5. give out the salary cheques

'I WAS PLANNING TO DO IT LATER'

Now present your own conversations.

(1) Do you/Would you (by any chance) know
Do you/Would you (by any chance) happen to know

(2) I don't think so.
Not as far as I know.

(3) Are you sure/certain/positive (about that)?

(4) I'm positive/certain/sure.
I'm absolutely positive/certain/sure.
I'm a hundred percent sure.
There's no doubt about it.

A. **Do you by any chance know**[1] when the American President is going to arrive?
B. Yes. As far as I know, he's going to arrive at 2:30.
A. Hmm. Somehow I thought he was going to arrive earlier than that.
B. **I don't think so.**[2]
A. **Are you sure?**[3]
B. Yes, **I'm positive.**[4] He arrives at 2:30.

1. at 9

2. at 3:30

3. at 7:45

4. late next month

5. in a fortnight

Now present your own conversations.

7.6 Unfulfilled intentions 'I forgot all about it.'

A. Oh dear! **Did you remember to**(1) feed the dog?
B. No, I didn't. I thought YOU were going to feed him!
A. Hmm. I WAS ... but **I forgot all about it.**(2)
B. Well, since the dog hasn't been fed yet, I suppose one of us should go and do it.
A. Okay. I'll do it.

(1) Did you (happen to) remember to _____?
You didn't (by any chance) remember to _____, did you?

(2) I forgot (all about it).
I completely/clean forgot.
It (completely) slipped my mind.
It went (clean) out of my mind.

1. put the dustbins out

2. set the table

3. turn the downstairs light off

4. do the washing

5. change the baby's nappy

'I FORGOT ALL ABOUT IT.'

Now present your own conversations.

(1) I won't be able to
I'm not going to be able to
I can't

(2) insisting that I
wanting me to

[stronger]
making me
forcing me to

(3) there's nothing I can do
about it
there's no way I can get
out of it
I can't get out of it

(4) We can (always) _____
We'll _____
Let's plan on _____ing
(Am.E.)

You have to work overtime today.

A. Hello! It's me again!
B. Hi! What's wrong?
A. Well, since I talked to you about an hour ago, I've found out that **I won't be able to**(1) go bowling with you as we had planned. Something important has just come up.
B. Oh?
A. Yes. My boss is **insisting that I**(2) work overtime today, and **there's nothing I can do about it.**(3) I hope you understand.
B. Of course I do. **We can always**(4) go bowling some other time.

You'd better tidy up your room.

my father

1. play tennis

I insist that you stay in bed until your temperature is normal.

my doctor

2. have lunch

You have to stay late and help with the stocktaking.

the store manager

3. play football

You've got to rerecord three songs.

my producer

4. have a drink

You've got to come to our school play.

my sister

5. go out

'I WON'T BE ABLE TO....'

Now present your own conversations.

7.8 INTERCHANGE: Discussing past plans and decisions
'I changed my mind.'

A. Well, if it isn't David Johnson!
B. Richard Peters! It's nice to see you again!
A. You know, David, I've been meaning to call you for a long time.
B. Me, too. How have you been?
A. Fine. How about yourself?
B. Oh, not too bad.
A. Tell me, David, last time I saw you, you were planning to study law, weren't you?
B. Yes, I was. But as it turned out, I changed my mind.
A. Oh, really? But **if I remember correctly,**[1] you were definitely going to. Whatever made you change your mind?
B. Well, it's a long story, and I don't want to bore you with all the details. But **what it boils down to is that**[2] I decided that it wasn't a very good idea. I decided to study medicine instead.
A. Medicine? That's very interesting.
B. And how about you? The last time we talked, didn't you tell me you were going to open your own estate agency?
A. That's right. I was. But things turned out differently.
B. But you seemed so determined to do that. What happened?
A. Well, it's very complicated, and I'm sure you don't want to know all the details. But **as it turned out,**[2] I decided that it just wasn't for me. So I decided to stay on at my old job instead.
B. Well, **a lot has happened**[3] since we last saw each other.
A. **It certainly has!**[4] You know, we should try to stay in touch.
B. Yes, we should. Let's have lunch together sometime soon.
A. Good idea.

(1)	If I remember correctly,	(2)	What it boils down to is that
	If I remember right,		The fact of the matter is that
	If my memory serves me,		As it turned out,
	Unless I'm mistaken,		

(3) a lot has happened
a lot has changed
there have been a lot of
    changes

(4) It   has!
    }certainly{
There   have!
You can say that again!
You're right.
I agree.
I'll say! (Am.E.)

A. Well, if it isn't _____ _____!
B. _____ _____! It's nice to see you again!
A. You know, _____, I've been meaning to call you for a long time.
B. Me, too. How have you been?
A. Fine. How about yourself?
B. Oh, not too bad.
A. Tell me, _____, last time I saw you, you were planning to _____, weren't you?
B. Yes, I was. But as it turned out, I changed my mind.
A. Oh, really? But **if I remember correctly,**(1) you were definitely going to. Whatever made you change your mind?
B. Well, it's a long story, and I don't want to bore you with all the details. But **what it boils down to is that**(2) I decided that it wasn't a very good idea. I decided to _____ instead.
A. _____? That's very interesting.
B. And how about you? The last time we talked, didn't you tell me you were going to _____?
A. That's right. I was. But things turned out differently.
B. But you seemed so determined to do that. What happened?
A. Well, it's very complicated, and I'm sure you don't want to know all the details. But **as it turned out,**(2) I decided that it just wasn't for me. So I decided to _____ instead.
B. Well, **a lot has happened**(3) since we last saw each other.
A. **It certainly has!**(4) You know, we should try to stay in touch.
B. Yes, we should. Let's have lunch together sometime soon.
A. Good idea.

You've just 'bumped into' somebody you haven't seen for a while. Create an original conversation using the model dialogue above as a guide. Feel free to adapt and expand the model in any way you wish.

UNIT 7 SUMMARY

Functions

Intention

Enquiring about . . .

Have you decided _____?

What are you doing *this afternoon?*

Expressing . . .

I'm going to _____.
I'm planning to _____.
I plan to _____.
I intend to _____.
I've decided to _____.

I'll _____ $\begin{cases} \text{right away.} \\ \text{right now.} \\ \text{as soon as I can.} \\ \text{at the first chance I get.} \end{cases}$

I've been thinking of _____ing.
I'm thinking of _____ing.
I've been thinking about _____ing.
I'm thinking about _____ing.

I've been meaning to _____ (for a long time).

I've thought about it for a long time.
I've given it a lot of thought.
I've given it a lot of (serious) consideration.

I've decided it's time to do it.

I haven't made up my mind yet.

I was planning to _____.
I was going to _____.
I intended to _____.
I thought I would _____.

I was determined to _____.

Invitations

Extending . . .

Would you like to join me?
Do you want to join me?
Would you be interested in joining me?

Accepting . . .

I'd like to.
I'd love to.
I'd like that.
I'd be happy to. (Am.E.)

Remembering/Forgetting

Enquiring about . . .

Did you (happen to) remember to _____?
You didn't (by any chance) remember to _____, did you?

Indicating . . .

I forgot (all about it).
I completely/clean forgot.
It (completely) slipped my mind.
It went (clean) out of my mind.

Certainty/Uncertainty

Enquiring about . . .

Are you positive/certain/sure (about that)?

Expressing certainty

I'm positive/certain/sure.
I'm absolutely positive/certain/sure.
I'm a hundred percent sure.
There's no doubt about it.

Expressing uncertainty

I don't think so.
Not as far as I know.
I'm not sure.
I'm not certain.
I don't know yet.

Surprise/Disbelief

Really?
Good heavens!
My word!
Gee!
Boy! }(Am.E.)
Wow!

Probability/Improbability

Expressing probability

I'll probably _____.
I'll most likely _____.

Possibility/Impossibility

Expressing possibility

I might _____.
I may _____.
I thought I might _____.
I thought I'd _____.

Agreement/Disagreement

Expressing agreement

I agree.
You're right.
You can say that again!
I'll say. (Am.E.)

Asking for and reporting information

Do you/Would you (by any chance) know _____?
Do you/Would you (by any chance) happen to know _____?

What's wrong?

Ability/Inability

Expressing inability

I won't be able to _____.
I'm not going to be able to _____.
I can't _____.

There's nothing I can do about it.
There's no way I can get out of it.
I can't get out of it.

Obligation

Expressing . . .

_____ is insisting that I _____.
_____ is wanting me to _____.
[stronger]
_____ is making me _____.
_____ is forcing me to _____.

Conversation strategies

Initiating a conversation

Hello! It's me!

Hi! It's me again!

Well, if it isn't _____!

Initiating a topic

You know, . . .

Focusing attention

What it boils down to is that . . .

The fact of the matter is that . . .

As it turned out, . . .

UNIT 8: OFFERING HELP AND EXPRESSING GRATITUDE

Present continuous
Present perfect passive
Imperative with present continuous
Simple past passive
Should I (offer)
I don't mind _____ing.
Would you like me to ...?

(1) Would you like me to
   _____?
   I'll _____, if you'd like.
   I'll/I'd be happy/glad to
   _____, if you'd like.

(2) Don't worry about it.
   That's okay/all right.

(3) No, really!
   Listen!
   (Oh,) come on!

(4) for a change
   for once

(5) It's very good of you.
   It's nice/kind of you to
      offer.
   That's (very) nice/kind of
      you.
   That would be nice.
   I appreciate it/that.
      (Am.E.)
   I'd appreciate it/that.
      (Am.E.)

A. **Would you like me to**(1) wash the dishes?
B. No. **Don't worry about it.**(2) I don't mind washing the dishes.
A. **No, really!**(3) You're always the one who does it. Let me do it **for a change.**(4)
B. Okay. Thanks. **It's very good of you.**(5)

1. water the plants

2. mow the lawn

3. put the dustbin out

4. defrost the refrigerator

5. feed the hamster

Now present your own conversations.

8.2 Offering help (2) 'I'd be glad to give you a hand.'

A. I see you're changing the oil.
B. Yes. It hasn't been changed for a long time.
A. **Want any help?**(1)
B. Yes. **If you don't mind.**(2)
A. No, not at all. **I'd be glad to give you a hand.**(3)
B. Thanks. I appreciate it.

(1) (Do you) want any help?
(Do you) need any help?
(Do you) want a hand?
(Do you) need a hand?
Can I help?
Can I give you a hand?

(2) If you don't mind.
If you wouldn't mind.
If it's no trouble.

(3) I'd be glad/happy to give
you a hand.
I'd be glad/happy to lend
a hand.
I'd be glad/happy to help.

1. clean the garage

2. wash the windows

3. paint the fence

4. sweep out the barn

5. bath Rover

'I'D BE GLAD TO GIVE YOU A HAND.'

Now present your own conversations.

8.3 Offering help (3)
'Would you like me to help you move that desk?'

(1) Would you like me to help you _____?
Do you want me to help you _____?
I'd be glad/happy to help you _____, (if you'd like).
Let me help you _____.
Would you like any help _____ing?
Would you like me to give you a hand _____ing?

(2) There's no sense in _____ing
There's no reason (for you) to _____
You don't have to _____
You shouldn't have to _____

(3) it's nice of you to offer
thanks for offering
I appreciate your offering (Am.E.)

(4) Look!
Listen!
Come on!

(5) trouble you
bother you
inconvenience you
put you to any trouble
put you out

A. **Would you like me to help you**(1) move that desk?
B. No, that's okay. I can move it myself.
A. Oh, come on! Let me give you a hand. **There's no sense in**(2) moving it yourself if I'm here to help.
B. Really, **it's nice of you to offer,**(3) but . . .
A. **Look!**(4) I insist! You're not moving that desk by yourself!
B. Well, okay. But I really don't want to **trouble you.**(5)
A. No trouble at all! Honestly! I'm happy to lend a hand.

1. lift that engine

2. carry those boxes

76

3. take down that sign

4. unload that lorry

5. put out those chairs

6. cut down that tree

7. adjust that TV aerial

8. change that wheel

9. sort those index cards

'WOULD YOU LIKE ME TO HELP YOU?'

Now present your own conversations.

8.4 Offering assistance (shops) 'Can I help you?'

(1) Can I help you?
Can I assist you?

(2) Is there anything/
something particular I
can help you find?
Is there anything/
something you're
looking for in particular?

(3) we're out of _____
we've run out of _____
we don't have any more
_____ in stock
our _____ is/are out of
stock

A. **Can I help you?**(1)
B. Not for the moment, thanks. I'm just looking.
A. **Is there anything particular I can help you find?**(2)
B. Well, actually, I'm looking for a digital watch.
A. Oh, I'm afraid **we're out of**(3) digital watches, but we
expect some in very soon. Is there anything else I can
help you with?
B. No thank you.

1. a size 40 jacket

2. a convertible sofa-bed

3. a size 16 shirt

4. a video cassette recorder

5. sugar-free chewing gum

Now present your own
conversations.

8.5 Offering assistance (accidents) 'Are you all right?'

A. Excuse me. Are you **all right?**(1)
B. Well, er ... I'm not sure.
A. What happened?
B. I was knocked down by someone on roller skates.
A. Oh, no! **Can I do anything to help?**(2)
B. **What?**(3)
A. Can I help? Should I **call an ambulance?**(4)
B. No, that's okay. I think I'll be all right.
A. Well, here. **Let me**(5) help you up.
B. Thanks. **You're very kind.**(6)
A. **Don't mention it.**(7)

(1) all right
okay

(2) Can I do anything to help?
Is there anything I can do
to help?
Can I help?

(3) What?
Sorry?

(4) call/get an ambulance
call/get a doctor
call/get the police

(5) Let me
I'll
Allow me to (Am.E.)

(6) You're very kind/nice.
That's (very) kind/nice of
you.

(7) Don't mention it.
Not at all.
You're welcome. (Am.E.)
Glad to be of help.
(Am.E.)
No problem. (Am.E.)

1. I've just been mugged.

2. I think I've sprained my
ankle.

3. I've just been hit by a car.

4. I fell off my bicycle.

5. I must have fainted.

Now present your own
conversations.

(1) it was nothing (at all)
(please) don't mention it

(2) No, I mean it!
No, really!
No, honestly!

(3) I'm very/most grateful (to you).
I really appreciate it. (Am.E.)
I appreciate it very much. (Am.E.)

(4) I'm glad I could help/do it/be of help.
(It was) my pleasure.
Don't mention it.

[informal]
Any time.

A. You know, I keep forgetting to thank you for lending me your calculator.
B. Oh, **it was nothing.**(1)
A. **No, I mean it!**(2) It was very nice of you to lend it to me. **I'm very grateful.**(3)
B. **I'm glad I could help.**(4)

1. lend me your car

2. recommend me for promotion

3. send me flowers when I was in hospital

4. create a new position in the company for my daughter

5. get me those cup-final tickets

Now present your own conversations.

8.7 INTERCHANGE: A speech of gratitude
'Words can't express . . .'

I'm very grateful to receive this 'Best Actress' award.
I can't begin to tell you how much I appreciate this honour.
There are many people I'd like to thank.

First of all,[1] I want to thank my director, Jack Robbins, for all his patience and encouragement.

I also want to express my gratitude to my acting teacher, Vincent Lewis, who taught me everything I know.

And finally, I want to express my appreciation to all of my friends for their **support,**[2] especially to Katherine Miller, for being there when I needed her.

This award means a great deal to me. Words can't express how **honoured**[3] I feel at this moment. Thank you very much.

[1] First of all, First and foremost, Most of all, Above all,	[2] support assistance encouragement guidance help inspiration advice	[3] honoured thrilled excited proud overwhelmed

I'm very grateful to receive this _____ award.
I can't begin to tell you how much I appreciate this honour.
There are many people I'd like to thank.

First of all,[1] I want to thank my _____ for _____.

I also want to express my gratitude to _____, who _____.

And finally, I want to express my appreciation to all of my friends for their _____,[2]
especially to _____, for _____.

This award means a great deal to me. Words can't express how _____[3] I feel at this
moment. Thank you very much.

You have just received an award. Make your acceptance speech using the model above as a guide. Feel free to adapt and expand the model in any way you wish.

UNIT 8 SUMMARY

Functions

Offering to do something

Would you like me to _____?
I'll _____, if you'd like.
I'll/I'd be happy/glad to _____, if
   you'd like.

Let me (_____).

Offering to help

Making an offer

(Do you) want any help?
(Do you) need any help?
(Do you) want a hand?
(Do you) need a hand?
Can I help?
Can I give you a hand?

Would you like me to help you
   _____?
Do you want me to help you _____?
I'd be glad/happy to help you _____,
   (if you'd like).
Let me help you _____.
Would you like any help _____ing?
Would you like me to give you a
   hand _____ing?

Can I do anything to help?
Is there anything I can do to help?
Can I help?

I'd be glad/happy to give you a hand.
I'd be glad/happy to lend a hand.
I'd be glad/happy to help.

Let me give you a hand.
I'm happy to lend a hand.

Let me _____.
I'll _____.
Allow me to _____. (Am.E.)

Can I help you?
Can I assist you?

Is there anything/something particular
   I can help you find?
Is there anything/something you're
   looking for in particular?

Is there anything else I can help you
   with?

Responding to an offer

If you don't mind.
If you wouldn't mind.
If it's no trouble.

I don't want to { trouble you.
bother you.
inconvenience you.
put you to any trouble.
put you out. }

Don't worry about it.
That's okay/all right.

Gratitude

Expressing . . .

Thanks (very much).
Thank you (very much).

I'm very grateful (to _____).

I want to thank _____.
I want to express my gratitude to
   _____.

I keep forgetting to thank you for
   _____.

Responding to . . .

Don't mention it.
Not at all.
It was nothing (at all).
You're welcome.
No problem. } (Am.E.)
Glad to be of help.

I'm glad I could help/do it/be of help.
(It was) my pleasure.
Don't mention it. [Informal]
Any time.

Appreciation

It's very good of you.
I appreciate your offering.
That's (very) nice/kind of you.
That would be nice.
Thanks for offering.
It's nice/kind of you to offer.
I appreciate it/that.
I'd appreciate it/that. } (Am.E.)

You're very kind/nice.

I'm very grateful (to _____).

I really appreciate it.
I appreciate it very much. } (Am.E.)

It was very nice of you (to _____).

I can't begin to tell you how much I
   appreciate _____.

I want to express my gratitude/
   appreciation to _____.

Persuading/Insisting

Listen!
Look!
(No,) really!
(No,) I mean it!
(No,) honestly!
(Oh,) come on!

I insist.

Let me, for a change.
Let me, for once.

There's no sense in _____ing.
There's no reason (for you) to _____.
You don't have to _____.
You shouldn't have to _____.

Attracting attention

Excuse me.

Conversation strategy

Initiating a topic

You know, . . .

82

UNIT 9: ASKING FOR AND GIVING PERMISSION

Could/can
Had better
Gerunds
Rather (+ 'didn't')
Mind (negative and interrogative)
Must/mustn't (prescriptive)

9.1 Enquiring about permission 'Is smoking **allowed here?**'

A. **Is** smoking **allowed**[1] here?
B. **Yes, it is.**[2]
A. Thanks.

A. **Are you allowed to** take pictures[1] here?
B. **No, you aren't.**[3]
A. Oh, okay. Thanks.

A. **Are people allowed to** park[1] here?
B. **Yes, they are.**[2]
A. Thanks.

A. **Do they allow** surfing[1] here?
B. **Not as far as I know.**[3]
A. Oh, okay. Thanks.

[1] Is _____ing allowed/permitted? Is it okay to _____?	[2] Yes, it is.	[3] No, it isn't.
Are you allowed to _____? Are people allowed to _____? Is one allowed to _____?	Yes, you are. Yes, they are. Yes, one is.	No, you aren't. No, you aren't. No, one isn't.
Do they allow _____ing? Do they allow people to _____?	Yes, they do. Yes, they do.	No, they don't. No, they don't.
	[less certain] I think so. I believe so. Yes, as far as I know.	[less certain] I don't think so. I don't believe so. Not as far as I know.

1. swim

2. camp

3. skate

4. feed the animals

5. dive

6. picnic

7. play a radio

8. play with a frisbee

9. sunbathe in the nude

Now present your own conversations.

85

9.2 Advising about permission
'I don't think you're allowed to pick the flowers.'

(1) Excuse me,
Pardon me, (Am.E.)

(2) I don't think you're
allowed to _____.
I don't think _____ing is
allowed.
I don't think people are/
one is allowed to _____.
I don't think they allow
people to _____.
I don't think they allow
you to _____.

(3) Well, now!
Goodness (me)!
Good gracious!
Good heavens!
(Well,) how about that!
(Am.E.)
(Well,) what do you know!
(Am.E.)
(Well,) how do you like
that! (Am.E.)
Isn't that something!
(Am.E.)

A. **Excuse me,**(1) but **I don't think you're allowed to**(2) pick the flowers.
B. Oh?
A. Yes. There's a sign here that says so.
B. Hmm. 'Please Don't Pick the Flowers.' **Well, now!**(3) I never even noticed it. Thanks for telling me.
A. You're welcome.

1.

3.

4.

5.

Now present your own conversations.

9.3 Asking for permission (1)
'Can I possibly have the car tonight?'

A. Could I ask you a favour?
B. Yes, of course.
A. **Can I possibly**[1] have the car tonight?
B. Hmm. **Let's see now.**[2] Well, **I think so.**[3] But you'd better check with your mother. I'm sure she won't **object to**[4] your having the car tonight, but it wouldn't hurt to ask.
A. Okay. Thanks. I'll check with her right away.

[1] Can/Could I (possibly) _____?
Can/Could I please _____?
May I (please) _____?
Is it all right/okay (with/by you) if I _____?
Would it be possible for me to _____?
I'd like to _____, if that's all right/okay (with/by you).

[2] Let's see now.
Let me think (for a minute).
Let me see.

[3] I think so.
I suppose so.
I don't see (any reason) why not.

[4] object to
have any objection to
mind

1. go home an hour early today

2. stay at Lucy's house tonight

3. borrow your TV until tomorrow

4. stay in my room a few hours after check-out time

5. grow flowers on my balcony

Now present your own conversations.

9.4 Asking for permission (2)
'Would you mind if I served leftovers for dinner?'

A. **Would you mind if I** served leftovers for dinner?[1]
B. **No, I wouldn't mind.**[2]
A. Are you sure? I mean if you'd rather I didn't I won't.
B. **Honestly.**[3] If you want to serve leftovers for dinner, it's **fine**[4] with me. **Go ahead.**[5]

A. **Is it all right with you if I** turn up the heating?[1]
B. **Of course.**[2]
A. Are you sure? I mean if you'd rather I didn't I won't.
B. **Honestly.**[3] If you want to turn up the heating, it's **fine**[4] with me. **Go ahead.**[5]

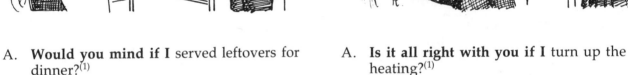

[1] Would you mind/object if I _____ed?
Would it bother you if I _____ed?
Do you mind if I _____? ⟶

[2] No, I wouldn't mind.
No, I don't mind.
(No,) of course not.
(No,) not at all.
No, it's all right/fine/okay with me.
No.

Is it all right/okay (with you) if I _____?
Would it be all right/okay (with/by you) if I _____ed?
I'd like to _____, if that's all right/okay (with/by you). ⟶

Of course.
Certainly.
By all means.
It's all right/okay with/by me.
Yes.
Sure. (Am.E.)

[3] Honestly.
Really.

[4] fine
all right
okay

[5] Go ahead.
Be my guest. (Am.E.)

1. Would you mind . . . ?

2. Is it all right with you . . . ?

3. Would it bother you . . . ?

4. I'd like to . . .

5. Do you mind . . . ?

6. Would you object . . . ?

7. Would it be all right with you . . . ?

8. Is it okay with you . . . ?

9. Would it bother you . . . ?

Now present your own conversations.

89

9.5 Asking for permission (3)
'Is it all right if I order steak for two?'

(1) Actually,
To be honest (with you),
To tell (you) the truth,

(2) I'd rather you didn't.
I'd prefer it if you didn't/
wouldn't.
I'd prefer you not to.

(3) You see
The reason is

A. Is it all right if I order steak for two?
B. **Actually,**(1) **I'd rather you didn't.**(2)
A. Oh, okay.
B. **You see**(3) ... I'm a vegetarian.
A. Oh, I'm sorry. I didn't know that.

1. Would you mind ...?

2. Do you mind ...?

3. Would it be okay ...?

4. Would you object ...?

5. Is it okay ...?

Now present your own conversations.

90

9.6 Obtaining permission 'How can I get his permission?'

the landlord

A. Could I ask you to change the lock on our door?
B. I'm afraid I can't do that without **permission from**[1] the landlord.
A. Oh? How can I get his permission?
B. Well, the best thing to do is to write a note asking him to **authorize me to**[2] change the lock on your door.
A. Okay. I'll do that.
B. I'm sorry. I don't mean to **make things difficult for you.**[3]
A. I understand.

[1] permission from
the permission of
the approval of
the consent of
the agreement of
a go-ahead from
an authorization from
(Am.E.)

[2] authorize me to _____
allow me to _____
permit me to _____
approve my _____ing
consent to my _____ing
agree to my _____ing
give the go-ahead for me
to _____

[3] make things difficult/
complicated for you
complicate things
give you a hard time
(Am.E.)

Mrs Field in the Maintenance Department

1. repair the ceiling in my office

Mr Thompson in the Accounts Department

2. give me an advance on my next month's salary

Mr Blackwell in the tutors' office

3. switch my main subject to accounting

the branch manager, Mrs Watkins

4. keep our mail at the post office while we're away

the board of directors

5. change my title to 'Senior Assistant-Manager'

'HOW CAN I GET PERMISSION?'

Now present your own conversations.

9.7 INTERCHANGE: What is and isn't allowed
'You mustn't under any circumstances use the fireplace.'

A. Before you sign the lease, do you have any questions?
B. Yes. Are we allowed to sublet the flat?
A. No. I'm afraid subletting isn't permitted.
B. I see. Well, is it all right to use the fireplace?
A. No. You mustn't under any circumstances use the fireplace.
B. Oh. Well, do you allow people to have pets?
A. No. That's out of the question. We don't allow anyone to have pets.
B. How about parking in front of the building?
A. I'm sorry. You're not supposed to park in front of the building.
B. Oh.
A. And before I forget, I should mention that you may not alter the premises in any way without permission. Now, do you have any other questions?
B. No, I think you've answered them all.

A. Before _____, do you have any questions?
B. Yes. Are we allowed to _____?
A. No. I'm afraid _____ing isn't permitted.
B. I see. Well, is it all right to _____?
A. No. You mustn't under any circumstances _____.
B. Oh. Well, do you allow people to _____?
A. No. That's out of the question. We don't allow anyone to _____.
B. How about _____ing?
A. I'm sorry. You're not supposed to _____.
B. Oh.
A. And before I forget, I should mention that you may not _____ without permission. Now, do you have any other questions?
B. No, I think you've answered them all.

1. Before you begin your first year here at Ilchester College ...

2. Before beginning your adventure holiday ...

3. Before you start your six weeks' basic training ...

4. Before your tour of The Republic of Grenomia gets underway ...

Create original conversations using the model dialogue on p. 92 as a guide. Feel free to adapt and expand the model is any way you wish.

UNIT 9 SUMMARY

Functions

Permission

Asking for ...

Can/Could I (possibly) _____?
Can/Could I please _____?
May I (please) _____?
Is it all right/okay (with you) if I
_____?
Would it be possible for me to _____?
I'd like to _____, if that's all right/
okay (with/by you).

Would you mind/object if I _____ed?
Would it bother you if I _____ed?
Do you mind if I _____?

Is it all right/okay (with/by you) if I
_____?
Would it be all right/okay (with you)
if I _____ed?
I'd like to _____, if that's all right/
okay (with you).

Granting ...

Of course.
Certainly.
By all means.
It's all right/okay with/by me.
Yes.
Sure. (Am.E.)

No, I wouldn't mind.
No, I don't mind.
(No,) of course not.
(No,) not at all.
No, it's all right/okay with me.
No.

Go ahead.
Be my guest. (Am.E.)

I think so.
I suppose so.
I don't see (any reason) why not.

If you want to _____,

it's { fine / all right / okay } with/by me.

Denying ...

I'd rather you didn't.
I'd prefer it if you didn't/wouldn't.
I'd prefer you not to.

_____ing isn't allowed.
You mustn't _____ (under any
circumstances).
We don't allow anyone to _____.
You're not supposed to _____.
You may not _____ (without
permission).

That's out of the question.

I can't do that without { permission from / the permission of / the approval of / the consent of / the agreement of / a go-ahead from / an authorization from (Am.E.) } _____.

Enquiring about permissibility

Is _____ing allowed/permitted?
Is it okay to _____?
Is it all right to _____?
Are you allowed to _____?
Are people allowed to _____?
Do they allow _____ing?
Do they allow people to _____?
Is one allowed to _____?

Indicating permissibility

I don't think _____ing is allowed.
I don't think you're allowed to
_____.
I don't think people are allowed to
_____.
I don't think they allow people to
_____.
I don't think they allow you to
_____.

Yes, _____ _____.
[less certain]
I think so.
I believe so.
Yes, as far as I know.

No, _____ _____.
[less certain]
I don't think so.
I don't believe so.
Not as far as I know.

Gratitude

Expressing ...

Thanks (for telling me).

Apologizing

(Oh,) I'm sorry.

{ I don't mean to / make things difficult/complicated / for you. / complicate things. / give you a hard time. (Am.E.) }

Attracting attention

Excuse me, ...
Pardon me, ... (Am.E.)

Surprise/Disbelief

Oh?
Well, now!
Goodness (me)!
Good gracious!
Good heavens!
(Well,) how about that!
(Well,) what do you know!
(Well,) how do you like that!
Isn't that something!
} (Am.E.)

Persuading/Insisting

Honestly.
Really.

Denying/Admitting

Admitting

You see ...
The reason is ...

Requests

Direct, polite

Could I ask you to _____?

Could I ask you a favour?

Conversation strategy

Hesitating

Hmm.

Let me think (for a minute).
Let me see.
Let's see now.

SCENES AND IMPROVISATIONS
Units 7–9

Who do you think these people are?
What do you think they're talking about?
Create conversations based on these scenes and act them out.

1.

2.

3.

4.

5.

7.

6.

8.

UNIT 10: INVITING

10.1 *Inviting/Accepting*
'How would you like to go to the zoo?'

10.2 *Inviting/Refusing*
'Would you be interested in seeing a film?'

10.3 *Inviting/Hesitating*
'Can you come?'

10.4 *Inviting/Arranging a time*
'How about 7 o'clock?'

10.5 *Interchange: Making a date*
'I'm free on Friday.'

Summary

Present perfect (negative — 'for')
Gerunds
Have to
Can (possibility)
Supposed to
Should (obligation)
Neither have I

10.1   Inviting/accepting   'How would you like to go to the zoo?'

(1) How would you like to
      _____?
      Would you like to _____?
      Do you want to _____?
      Would you be interested
      in _____ing?
      How about _____ing?
      Let's _____.

(2) I'd love to.
      I'd like to.
      That sounds great/fun/
        terrific/wonderful.
      That would be great/
        terrific/wonderful/fun.
      I'd be happy to/glad to.
        (Am.E.)
      I'd like that. (Am.E.)
      That sounds like fun.
        (Am.E.)
      [stronger]
      I'd be delighted to

(3) a nice idea
      a good idea
      a nice thing to do
      a nice/good way to spend
        the day

A.   **How would you like to**(1) go to the zoo this Sunday?
B.   **I'd love to.**(2) I haven't gone to the zoo for a long time.
A.   Neither have I. That's why I thought going to the zoo
     might be **a nice idea.**(3)

1. go to the cinema

2. play a game of tennis

3. go sailing

4. go for a drive in
        the country

5. pick strawberries

Now present your own
conversations.

98

10.2 Inviting/refusing
'Would you be interested in seeing a film?'

A. **If you're not busy,**[1] **would you be interested in**[2] seeing a film with me this Saturday?
B. I'd love to, but I **can't.**[3] **I have to**[4] study for my college entrance exams.
A. That's a pity.
B. Thanks for **asking,**[5] though. Maybe we can see a film some other time.

[1] If you're not busy,
    If you're free,
    If you don't have any other plans,

[2] Would you (by any chance) be interested in _____ing?
    You wouldn't (by any chance) be interested in _____ing, would you?

[3] can't
    won't be able to

[4] I have to
    I've got to
    I'm supposed to
    I must

[5] asking (me)
    inviting me
    the invitation

1. go to my cousin's wedding

2. help my parents with the 'spring cleaning'

3. take care of my little sister

4. take part in our school concert

5. work on my science project

Now present your own conversations.

(1) Can you come?
Do you think you can come?
Do you think you'll be able to come?
Would you be able to come?
Can you make it?
Do you think you can make it?

(2) I'll check and let you know.
Let me check and get back to you.

(3) I'll do my best.
I'll try as hard as I can.

I'm organizing a company picnic for this Saturday.

A. I'm organizing a company picnic for this Saturday. **Can you come?**(1)
B. I'd love to, but I'm not sure that I can. I think I'm supposed to work overtime.
A. That's a shame. Is there any chance you could possibly get out of working overtime?
B. I'm not sure. **I'll check and let you know.**(2)
A. Okay, but please try to come. It won't be much of a company picnic without you!
B. It's nice of you to say that. **I'll do my best.**(3)

I'm having a party this Saturday night.

1. baby-sit

I'm planning a family get-together for April 20th.

2. speak at my firm's annual meeting

I'm giving a party for my husband's birthday on Friday night.

3. be on duty

I'm organizing a football match for this Saturday afternoon.

4. help my brother paint the house

We're holding a fete on the first Saturday in June.

5. collect for 'the heart fund'

'CAN YOU COME?'

Now present your own conversations.

A. **We'd like to invite you and your wife round**[1] for dinner this Saturday evening. Would you be able to come?
B. This Saturday evening?
A. Yes, and we hope you'll be able to join us.
B. **Thank you for the invitation.**[2] We'd be **very happy**[3] to come.
A. Good.
B. What time **should we come?**[4]
A. **How about 7:00?**[5]
B. 7:00? Fine. We'll be looking forward to it.

[1] We'd like to invite you and your wife round/over
We'd like to have you and your wife round/over
We'd like you and your wife to join us
We'd like you and your wife to be our guests (Am.E.)

[2] Thank you/Thanks for the invitation.
Thank you/Thanks for inviting us.
It's very nice of you to invite us.

[3] very happy/glad
pleased
delighted

[4] should we come/arrive/get there
are we invited (for)
should we aim/plan to arrive/get there

[5] How about 7:00?
Is 7:00 convenient/all right?
Would 7:00 be convenient/all right?
How does 7:00 sound? (Am.E.)

1. you and your husband

3. you and your wife

4. you and your fiancé

5. you and your fiancée

'HOW ABOUT...?'

Now present your own conversations.

10.5 INTERCHANGE: Making a date
'I'm free on Friday.'

A. I'd love to continue this conversation, but I really must go now. I have to get back to the office.
B. Well, let's get together soon.
A. Okay. Would you like to have lunch one day next week?
B. I'd love to. How about Monday?
A. Hmm. I'm afraid I can't make it on Monday. I've got to fly to Glasgow on business.
B. Well unfortunately, I'm tied up on Tuesday. I'm supposed to have lunch with an important overseas visitor and I don't think I can get out of it. Are you free on Wednesday?
A. Wednesday? Let's see. Hmm. I think I've already got an appointment on Wednesday. Oh, yes! I'm going to the dentist.
B. Well, I'm afraid Thursday is out for me. I'm expected to attend a meeting of our personnel committee and it's very important for me to be there.
A. So that leaves Friday. I'm free on Friday. How about you?
B. Friday sounds fine. Where shall we meet?
A. You know, I really must be going now or I'll be very late. Can you phone me tomorrow and we'll decide?
B. Fine. We'll decide then.
A. Sorry I have to rush off like this.
B. That's okay. I understand.
A. Goodbye.
B. Bye.

A. I'd love to continue this conversation, but I really must go now. I have to _____.

B. Well, let's get together soon.

A. Okay. Would you like to _____ one day next week?

B. I'd love to. How about Monday?

A. I'm afraid I can't make it on Monday. I've got to _____.

B. Well unfortunately, I'm tied up on Tuesday. I'm supposed to _____ and I don't think I can get out of it. Are you free on Wednesday?

A. Wednesday? Let's see. Hmm. I think I've already got an appointment on Wednesday. Oh, yes! I'm _____.

B. Well, I'm afraid Thursday is out for me. I'm expected to _____ and it's very important for me _____.

A. So that leaves Friday. I'm free on Friday. How about you?

B. Friday sounds fine. Where shall we meet?

A. You know, I really must be going now or I'll be very late. Can you phone me tomorrow and we'll decide?

B. Fine. We'll decide then.

A. Sorry I have to rush off like this.

B. That's okay. I understand.

A. Goodbye.

B. Bye.

You are talking to a friend when you realize you have to go or you'll be late. Create an original conversation using the model dialogue as a guide. Feel free to adapt and expand the model in any way you wish.

UNIT 10 SUMMARY

Functions

Ability/Inability

Enquiring about ...

Can you _____?
Is there any chance you could
  (possibly) _____?
Would you be able to _____?

Expressing inability

I can't.
I won't be able to.

I'm not sure (that) I can.

I can't make it on _____.
I'm tied up on _____.

Invitations

Extending ...

How would you like to _____?
Would you like to _____?
Do you want to _____?
Would you be interested in _____ing?
How about _____ing?
Let's _____.

Would you (by any chance) be
  interested in _____ing?
You wouldn't (by any chance) be
  interested in _____ing, would you?

We'd like to invite you (and _____)
  round/over for _____.
We'd like to have you (and _____)
  round/over for _____.
We'd like you (and _____) to join us
  for _____.
We'd like you (and _____) to be our
  guest(s) for _____. (Am.E.)

Can you come?
Do you think you can come?
Do you think you'd be able to come?
Would you be able to come?
Can you make it?
Do you think you can make it?

Please try to come.

We hope you'll be able to join us.

If you're not busy, ...
If you're free, ...
If you don't have any other plans, ...

Accepting ...

I'd love to.
I'd like to.
That sounds great/terrific/fun/
  wonderful.
That would be great/terrific/
  wonderful/fun.
I'd be happy to/glad to.
I'd like that.   }(Am.E.)
That sounds like fun.
[stronger]
I'd be delighted to.

We'd be {very happy / very glad / pleased / delighted} to come.

We'll be looking forward to it.

Thanks/Thank you for {asking. / inviting me. / the invitation.}

It's (very) nice of you to invite me.

Declining ...

I'd love to, but I can't.
I'd love to, but I won't be able to.

Obligation

Expressing ...

I have to _____.
I've got to _____.
I'm supposed to _____.
I must _____.
I'm expected to _____.

I don't think I can get out of it.

I'm tied up on _____.
I've got an appointment on _____.

Leave Taking

I'd love to continue this conversation,
  but ...

I (really) must be going.

Goodbye.
Bye.

Sorry I have to rush off like this.

Conversation strategy

Checking and indicating
understanding

*Checking one's own
  understanding*

This Saturday evening?
7:00?

104

UNIT 11: REQUESTING

Summary

> Would/could (in requests)
> Imperatives
> Indirect questions
> Would you mind _____ing?/if ...?
> Have to/have got to (obligation)

11.1 Simple requests (1) 'Please tidy up your room.'

(1) Please _____.
Could you (please) _____?
Will you (please) _____?
Would you (please) _____?
I'd like you to _____.
I wish you would _____.
(Am.E.)

(2) What did you ask me to do?
What did you say?
What was that?

(3) Okay.
All right.
Sure. (Am.E.)

A. Charles. **Please**(1) tidy up your room before dinner.
B. Sorry, I didn't hear you. **What did you ask me to do?**(2)
A. I asked you to tidy up your room before dinner.
B. **Okay.**(3)

1. wind up the car windows

2. help me fold these towels

3. change your clothes before the guests arrive

4. take the dog for a walk before you leave for work

5. give me a hand opening this jar of pickles

Now present your own conversations.

106

11.2 Simple requests (2)
'I'd like you to retype the letter to Mr Casey.'

A. George, **I'd like you to**(1) retype the letter to Mr Casey.
B. The letter to Mr Casey?
A. Yes. And while you're at it, please get me the Jones file.
B. **Certainly.**(2) I'll do it **right away.**(3)

(1) I'd like you to _____.
Please _____.
Can you (please) _____?
Will you (please) _____?
Would you (please) _____?
I wish you would _____.
(Am.E.)

(2) Certainly.
Of course.

(3) right away
straight away
at once
immediately

1. put these glasses through the dishwasher
get some more spoons and forks

2. take Mr Anderson's blood pressure
check his temperature

3. order me a ham sandwich
phone my dentist and change my appointment

4. take these boxes to the stockroom
check our supply of glue

5. put these fan letters in my dressing room
phone ETV and cancel my appearance on 'The Mike Williams Show'

'I'D LIKE YOU TO...'

Now present your own conversations.

11.3 Requesting a favour 'Could you do me a favour?'

give me a lift home?

lend me your vacuum cleaner?

A. **Could you do me a favour?**[1]
B. What is it?
A. **Could you possibly**[2] give me a lift home?
B. **All right.**[3]
A. Are you sure? I don't want to **inconvenience you.**[4]
B. **No problem.**[5] **I'd be glad to.**[6]
A. Thanks. **I'm most grateful.**[7]

A. **Could you do me a favour?**[1]
B. What is it?
A. **Would you mind**[2] lending me your vacuum cleaner?
B. **No, I wouldn't mind.**[3]
A. Are you sure? I don't want to **inconvenience you.**[4]
B. **No problem.**[5] **I'd be glad to.**[6]
A. Thanks. **I'm most grateful.**[7]

---

[1] Could you do me a favour?
Could I ask you a favour?
Could you do a favour for me?

- - - - - - - - - - - - - -

[2] Could you possibly _____?
Could you (please) _____?
Could I (possibly) ask you to _____?
Would you be willing to _____?
Do you think you'd be able to _____?
I wonder if you could (possibly) _____.

Would you mind _____ing?

[3] All right.
Okay.
Of course.
Sure. (Am.E.)

No, I wouldn't mind.
No, of course not.
No, not at all.

- - - - - - - - - - - - - -

[4] inconvenience you
trouble you
bother you
put you to any trouble
put you out

[5] No problem.
No trouble at all.

[7] I'm most grateful.
I (really) appreciate it.
(Am.E.)

[6] I'd be glad/happy to.
(It would be) a pleasure.

1. Could I ask you to ...?

2. Would you mind ...?

3. Would you be willing to ...?

4. Would you mind ...?

5. Would you mind ...?

6. Do you think you'd be able to ...?

7. I wonder if you could ...

Now present your own conversations.

11.4 Polite requests
'Would you be willing to change seats with me?'

A. Excuse me. **Would you be willing to**[1] change seats with me?
B. Change seats?
A. Er ... yes. If you would, **I'd be most grateful.**[3]
B. **Of course.**[2]
A. Oh, thank you.
B. **That's all right.**[4]

A. Excuse me. **Would you mind**[1] dropping me off in front of my house?
B. In front of your house?
A. Er ... yes. If you wouldn't mind, **I'd be most grateful.**[3]
B. **No, I wouldn't mind.**[2]
A. Oh, thank you.
B. **That's all right.**[4]

---

[1] Would you be willing to _____?
Would you be kind enough to _____?
Could you possibly _____? ⟶

[2] Of course.
Yes, I would.
All right.
I'd be glad/happy to.
Sure. (Am.E.)
[informal]
Okay.

Would you mind _____ing?
Would you mind if I asked you to _____? ⟶

No, I wouldn't (mind).
Not at all.
[informal]
No problem.

[3] I'd be most grateful.
I'd (really) appreciate it.

[4] That's all right.
Not at all.
(Please) don't mention it.
I'm glad/happy to do it.
My pleasure. ⎫
You're welcome. ⎭ (Am.E.)
[informal]
No problem.

1. Could you possibly ...?

2. Would you mind ...?

3. Would you be kind enough to ...?

4. Would you mind if I asked you to ...?

5. Would you be willing to ...?

6. Would you mind ...?

7. Would you mind if I asked you to ...?

Now present your own conversations.

111

11.5 Refusing a request 'I'd like to, but I'm afraid I can't.'

(1) I'd like to
I'd love to
I'd do so, willingly

(2) I have to
I've got to
I'm supposed to
I must

(3) I'm (really) sorry.
I'm awfully sorry.
I feel terrible.

A. Could I possibly ask you to help me get this refrigerator up the stairs?
B. **I'd like to,**(1) but I'm afraid I can't. **I have to**(2) avoid lifting heavy things.
A. Oh, okay.
B. **I'm really sorry.**(3)
A. Don't worry about it. I understand.

1. Would you be willing to ...?

2. I wonder if you could ...

3. Would you mind ...?

4. Would you mind if I asked you to ...?

5. Do you think you'd be able to ...?

Now present your own conversations.

11.6 Requesting directions and instructions
'Could you tell me how to get to the post office?'

- Go to the corner and turn right.
- Go straight on to the High Street.
- Turn left, carry on and you'll see the post office next to the bank.

A. **Could you tell me**[1] how to get to the post office?
B. Certainly. Go to the corner and turn right. Go straight on to the High Street. Turn left, carry on and you'll see the post office next to the bank. **Have you got that?**[2]
A. I think so. **Let me see.**[3]
First, I go to the corner and turn right.
B. **Uh-huh.**[4]
A. Then I walk straight on to the High Street. Right?
B. **Um-hmm.**[4]
A. And then I . . . Hmm. I've forgotten the last part. What do I do after that?
B. You turn left, carry on and you'll see the post office next to the bank.
A. Okay.
B. Do you think you've got it now?
A. I think so. Thanks very much.

---

[1] Could you (please/possibly) tell me
Do you/Would you (by any chance) know
Can you (please) tell me
Would you (possibly/by any chance) be able to tell me

[2] (Have you) got that?
Do you follow me?
Okay?

[3] Let me see.
Let me see if I understand.
Let me see if I've got that (right).

[4] Uh-huh.
Um-hmm.
Yes.
(That's) right.

A. **Could you tell me**[1] how to _____?
B. Certainly. _____.
_____.

Have you got that?[2]
A. I think so. **Let me see.**[3]
First, I _____.
B. **Uh-huh.**[4]
A. Then I _____. Right?
B. **Um-hmm.**[4]
A. And then I . . . Hmm. I've forgotten the last part. What do I do after that?
B. You _____.
A. Okay.
B. Do you think you've got it now?
A. I think so. Thanks very much.

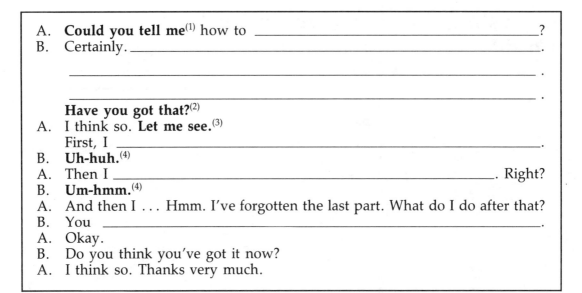

• Pick up the receiver.

• Put in the money.

• Wait for the dialling tone and dial.

1. use this telephone

• Pick up the nozzle.

• Put the nozzle in the petrol tank.

• Press the handle to start the petrol flowing.

2. work the petrol pump

• Use the jack to raise the car.

• Unscrew the bolts and take off the flat tyre.

• Put on the new tyre, put the bolts on tight, and lower the car.

3. change a flat tyre

• Turn round and drive down this road until you get to a big crossroads.

• Turn left and drive about three miles until you get on to the motorway.

• Take the motorway north to exit 27.

4. get to the airport

'COULD YOU TELL ME HOW TO...?'

Now present your own conversations.

11.7 INTERCHANGE: Requesting via messages
'Please ask him to bring a few bottles of soda to the party tonight.'

A. Hello. **Can I speak to**(1) Larry, **please?**
B. I'm afraid Larry isn't here at the moment. **Can I take a message?**(2)
A. Yes. This is his friend Bob **calling.**(3) Please **ask**(4) him to bring a few bottles of soda to the party tonight.
B. Okay. **Just a minute.**(5) **I'm writing this down.**(6) 'Bob called. You should bring a few bottles of soda to the party tonight.' Is that it?
A. Yes, that's it. You might ask him to call me back if he has time.
B. All right. I'll give him the message.
A. Thanks very much.
B. Goodbye.
A. Goodbye.

A. Hello. **Can I speak to**(1) _____, **please?**
B. I'm afraid _____ isn't here at the moment. **Can I take a message?**(2)
A. Yes. This is _____ **calling.**(3) Would you please **ask**(4) _____ to _____ _____?
B. Okay. **Just a minute.**(5) **I'm writing this down.**(6) '_____ called. You should _____ _____.' Is that it?
A. Yes, that's it. You might ask him/her to call me back if he/she has time.
B. All right. I'll give him/her the message.
A. Thanks very much.
B. Goodbye.
A. Goodbye.

---

(1) Can/Could I speak to _____ (please)?
I'd like to speak to _____ (please), (if he's/she's there).
Is _____ there?

(2) Can I take a message?
Can I give him/her a message?
Would you like to leave a message (for him/her)?

(3) calling
speaking

(4) ask
tell

(5) Just a minute.
Just a/one moment.
Hold on a minute/moment.

(6) I'm writing this down.
I'm taking this down.

Create an original telephone conversation using the model dialogue above as a guide. Feel free to adapt and expand the model in any way you wish.

UNIT 11 SUMMARY

Functions

Requests

Direct, polite

Please _____.
Could you (please) _____?
Can you (please) _____?
Will you (please) _____?
Would you (please) _____?
I'd like you to _____.
I wish you would _____. (Am.E.)

Could you do me a favour?
Could I ask you a favour?
Could you do a favour for me?

Would you please ask/tell _____ to
    _____?

Direct, more polite

Could you possibly _____?
Could you (please) _____?
Could I (possibly) ask you to _____?
Would you be willing to _____?
Do you think you'd be able to _____?
I wonder if you could (possibly)

    _____.
Would you mind _____ing?

Less direct, very polite

Would you be kind enough to _____?
Would you mind if I asked you to
    _____?

Responding to requests

Okay.
All right.
Certainly.
Of course.
I'd be glad/happy to.
Sure. (Am.E.)
[Informal]
Okay.

No, I wouldn't mind.
No, of course not.
No, not at all.
[Informal]
No problem.
No trouble at all.

Attracting attention

Charles.

Excuse me.

Gratitude

Expressing . . .

Thanks (very much).
I'm most grateful.
I (really) appreciate it. (Am.E.)

Responding to . . .

That's all right.
Not at all.
Don't mention it.
(I'm) glad to do it.
You're welcome. ⎫
My pleasure. ⎬ (Am.E.)

Ability/Inability

Expressing inability

I'd like to/love to, but I'm afraid I
    can't.
I'd do so willingly, but I'm afraid I
    can't.

Obligation

Expressing . . .

I have to _____.
I've got to _____.
I'm supposed to _____.
I must _____.

Apologizing

I'm (really) sorry.
I'm awfully sorry.
I feel terrible.

Offering to do something

Can I take a message?
Can I give him/her a message?
Would you like to leave a message
    (for him/her)?

Asking for and reporting information

Could you (please/possibly) tell me
    _____?
Do you/Would you (by any chance)
    know _____?
Can you (please) tell me _____?
Would you (possibly/by any chance)
    be able to tell me _____?

Directions/Location

Asking for directions

Could you tell me how to get
    to _____?

Giving directions

Go to _____.
Turn _____.
Walk _____.
Carry on _____.

Willingness

I'll do it right away.
I'll do it straight away.
I'll do it at once.
I'll do it immediately.

Conversation strategies

Asking for repetition

Sorry, I didn't hear you.

What did you ask me to do?
What did you say?
What was that?

Checking and indicating understanding

Checking another person's understanding

(Have you) got that?
Do you follow me?
Okay?
Do you think you've got it now?

Checking one's own understanding

Let me see.
Let me see if I understand.
Let me see if I've got that (right).

Change seats?

Indicating understanding

Uh-huh.
Um-hmm.
Yes.
(That's) right.

Initiating a conversation

Can/Could I speak to _____, (please)?
(Hello.) I'd like to speak to _____ (please), (if he's/she's there).
Is _____ there?

SCENES AND IMPROVISATIONS
Units 10–11

Who do you think these people are?
What do you think they're talking about?
Create conversations based on these scenes and act them out.

1.

2.

3.

4.

5.

6.

7.

8.

UNIT 12: SUGGESTIONS, ADVICE AND WARNINGS

12.1 *Making suggestions* (1)
   'How about Tooth-brite?'

12.2 *Making suggestions* (2)
   'What if we went for a ride in the country?'

12.3 *Advising* (1)
   'I (strongly) advise you to take physics.'

12.4 *Advising* (2)
   'I think you should see a doctor.'

12.5 *Advising* (3)
   'Have you considered putting the baby in a day-care centre?'

12.6 *Warning*
   'You'd better get out of the way.'

12.7 *Interchange: Making recommendations*
   'You ought to see the Palace at Versailles.'

   Summary

   Gerunds
   I don't think I'm in the mood for/to . . .
   What if (+ simple past)
   Present perfect (negative − 'for')
   First conditional (− 'might')
   Present perfect continuous
   Should (advice)
   Passives
   Past perfect
   Ought to (advice)
   Suggest (that)
   Be sure to
   Had better (advice)

12.1 Making suggestions (1) 'How about Tooth-brite?'

(1) Do you have any suggestions?
Can you recommend one?
What do you suggest/recommend?

(2) How about _____?
What about _____?
I/I'd suggest _____.
I/I'd recommend _____.

(3) Everybody says
People say
Everybody tells me
Most people say
I hear
They say

A. I'm looking for a fresh-tasting toothpaste. **Do you have any suggestions?**(1)
B. A fresh-tasting toothpaste. Hmm. Well, **how about**(2) Tooth-brite?
A. Tooth-brite?
B. Yes. I think you'll like it. **Everybody says**(3) it's very fresh-tasting.
A. Okay. Thanks for the suggestion.

1.

2.

3.

4.

5.

Now present your own conversations.

12.2 Making suggestions (2)
'What if we went for a ride in the country?'

go window-shopping?

go for a ride in the country?

A. What do you want to do today?
B. I don't know. Do you have any **ideas?**(1)
A. Well, **how about**(2) going window-shopping?
B. Oh, I don't know. **I don't think I'm in the mood to**(3) go window-shopping. Any other suggestions?
A. Well, let's see. **What if we**(2) went for a ride in the country?
B. **Hmm.**(4) **Good idea.**(5) We haven't gone for a ride in the country **for ages.**(6)

(1) ideas
suggestions
thoughts

(2) How about _____ing?
What about _____ing?
Let's _____.
What if we _____ed?
Why don't we _____?
We could (always) _____.

(3) I don't think I'm in the
mood to _____/for
_____ing.
I don't really feel like
_____ing.

(4) Hmm.
[more excited]
Hey! } (Am.E.)
Say! }

(5) (That's a/What a) good
idea.
(That's a/What a) good
suggestion.
That sounds good/great.
That sounds like a good
idea.

(6) for ages
for a long time

play squash?

go bowling?

1.

go fishing

ride our bikes
along the river?

2.

play bridge with
the Carters?

go to the
theatre?

3.

saw firewood?

drive into town?

4.

do some
baking?

go to the
beach?

5.

'WHAT IF...?'

Now present your own
conversations.

123

12.3 Advising (1) 'I (strongly) advise you to take physics.'

(1) I (strongly) advise you to
_____.
I urge you to _____.
I recommend that you
_____.
I recommend _____ing.

(2) important
necessary

(3) Definitely!
Absolutely!
Without question!
No doubt about it.

(4) you might _____
you could (possibly)
_____
you could/would run the
risk of _____ing
there's a chance you
might/could _____

(5) warning
advice

careers teacher

A. As your careers teacher, **I strongly advise you to**(1) take physics.
B. Do you really think it's **important?**(2)
A. **Definitely!**(3) If you don't, **you might**(4) have trouble getting into the medical faculty.
B. Oh. Well, thank you for the **warning.**(5)

doctor

1. go on a low-fat diet
   have a heart attack some day

probation officer

2. join one of the training programmes
   find yourself back inside again

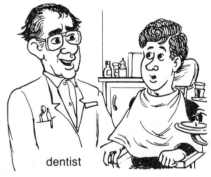

dentist

3. brush your teeth after every meal
   lose your teeth some day

bank manager

4. take out a smaller loan
   have difficulty meeting the monthly payments

stockbroker

5. sell all your shares in Grenomia Mining, Limited
   lose a lot of money

'I (STRONGLY) ADVISE YOU TO...'

Now present your own conversations.

12.4 Advising (2) 'I think you should see a doctor.'

A. **You seem troubled.**[1] Is anything **the matter?**[2]
B. Yes, as a matter of fact, I've been having this pain in my chest lately.
A. Well, can I **offer you some advice?**[3]
B. Yes. What?
A. **I think you should**[4] see a doctor.
B. You're probably right.

[1] You seem troubled/upset.
   You don't seem to be
     yourself today.

[2] the matter
   wrong
   bothering you

[3] offer you some advice
   give you a piece of advice
   make a suggestion

[4] I think you should/ought
    to _____.
   I/I'd suggest that you

    _____.
   I/I'd suggest _____ing.
   If I were you, I'd _____.
   It seems to me (that) you
    should _____.
   Don't you think you
    should _____?
   Don't you think it would/
    might be a good idea to
    _____?
   Be sure to _____.

1. take him to court

2. tell Miss Evans

3. make a complaint through the union

4. take a few days off

5. be frank with him

Now present your own conversations.

12.5 Advising (3) 'Have you considered putting the baby in a day-care centre?'

(1) Have you considered
_____ing?
Have you thought of
_____ing?
Have you thought about
_____ing?
You might consider
_____ing.
Why don't you _____?
You could (always) _____.
How about _____ing?
What about _____ing?
It might be a good idea to
_____.
What if you were to
_____?

(2) I hadn't thought of that.
That hadn't occurred to
me.

A. I need your advice.
B. Of course. What is it?
A. I've been offered a good full-time job, and I don't know what to do about it.
B. Well, **have you considered**(1) putting the baby in a day-care centre?
A. Hmm. **I hadn't thought of that.**(2)

1. move to another department

2. look for a flat in town

126

3. join 'Weight watchers'

4. ask your landlord to call a pest controller

5. take a year off

6. get a loan from the bank

7. see a doctor

8. go to evening classes

9. separate for a little while

Now present your own conversations.

12.6 Warning 'You'd better get out of the way!'

(1) (Be) careful!
Look out!
Watch out!
Mind out!

(2) Eh?
What?

[more polite]
Sorry?
Excuse me?
Pardon (me)? } (Am.E.)

(3) Thanks for the warning.
Thanks for warning me.

A. **Careful!**(1)
B. **Eh?**(2)
A. You'd better get out of the way!
B. Oh?
A. Yes. That forklift is coming toward you! You might get run over!
B. **Thanks for the warning.**(3)

A. **Careful!**(1)
B. **What?**(2)
A. You'd better not walk over there!
B. Oh?
A. Yes. The floor is wet! You might slip!
B. **Thanks for the warning.**(3)

1. get hurt

2. get hit

3. get knocked down by a waiter

4. get bitten

5. get fired

Now present your own conversations.

12.7 INTERCHANGE: Making recommendations
'You ought to see the Palace at Versailles.'

A. You've been to Paris, haven't you?
B. Yes. As a matter of fact, I used to live in Paris.
A. Well, I'm planning to go there soon, and I was wondering if you could recommend some things to do.
B. Of course. You should definitely go to Notre Dame. You also ought to see the Palace at Versailles. And you must visit The Louvre.
A. Those sound like excellent suggestions. Can you recommend any good places to eat?
B. Yes. Try to book a table at 'Maxim's'. And if you go there, I suggest you order the duck. It's delicious.
A. That sounds good.
B. Oh, and one more thing. Be sure to get someone to take your picture in front of the Eiffel Tower.
A. I'll do that.
B. Is there anything else I can tell you about?
A. I don't think so. You've been very helpful. Thanks a lot.
B. Send me a postcard, will you?
A. I certainly will.

A. You've been to _____, haven't you?
B. Yes. As a matter of fact, I used to live in _____.
A. Well, I'm planning to go there soon, and I was wondering if you could recommend some things to do.
B. Of course. You should definitely go to _____ _____. You also ought to see _____. And you must visit _____.
A. Those sound like excellent suggestions. Can you recommend any good places to eat?
B. Yes. Try to book a table at '_____'. And if you go there, I suggest you order the _____. It's delicious.
A. That sounds good.
B. Oh, and one more thing. Be sure to get someone to take your picture in front of _____.
A. I'll do that.
B. Is there anything else I can tell you about?
A. I don't think so. You've been very helpful. Thanks a lot.
B. Send me a postcard, will you?
A. I certainly will.

You're planning a trip. Create an original conversation using the model dialogue above as a guide and using functional expressions found throughout this unit. Feel free to adapt and expand the model in any way you wish.

UNIT 12 SUMMARY

Functions

Advice/Suggestions

Asking for ...

I need your advice.

Do you have any suggestions/
   recommendations/ideas/thoughts?
What do you suggest/recommend?

Can you recommend _____?
I was wondering if you could
   recommend _____.

Any other suggestions?

Offering ...

Can I offer you some advice?
Can I give you a piece of advice?
Can I make a suggestion?

I (strongly) advise you to _____.
I urge you to _____.
I recommend that you _____.
I recommend _____ing.

You should (definitely) _____.
You ought to _____.
You must _____.
Be sure to _____.

I think you should/ought to _____.
I/I'd suggest that you _____.
I/I'd suggest _____ing.
If I were you, I'd _____.
It seems to me (that) you should
   _____.
Don't you think you should _____?
Don't you think it would/might be a
   good idea to _____?
Be sure to _____.
How about _____?
What about _____?
I/I'd suggest _____.
I/I'd recommend _____.

How about _____ing?
What about _____ing?
Let's _____.
What if we _____ed?
Why don't we _____?
We could (always) _____.

Have you considered _____ing?
Have you thought of/about _____ing?
You might consider _____ing.
Why don't you _____?
You could (always) _____.
How about _____ing?
What about _____ing?
It might be a good idea to _____.
What if you were to _____?

Responding to ...

(That's a/What a) good idea.
(That's a/What a) good suggestion.
That sounds good/great.
That sounds like a good idea.

I hadn't thought of that.
That hadn't occurred to me.

Warning

If you don't (_____), _____.

(Be) careful!
Look out!
Watch out!
Mind out!

(You'd better) *get out of the way!*
(You'd better) stay away from the
   _____!
(You'd better) keep clear of the
   _____!
You'd better not _____!
Don't _____!

You might _____.

Gratitude

Expressing ...

Thanks/Thank you for _____.

Thanks a lot.

Want/Desire

Enquiring about ...

What do you want to do today?

Expressing ...

I don't think I'm in the mood to
   _____/for _____ing.
I don't really feel like _____ing.

Possibility/Impossibility

Expressing ...

You might _____.
You could (possibly) _____.
You could/would run the risk of
   _____ing.
There's a chance you might/could
   _____.

Asking for and reporting information

Is anything { the matter?
             { wrong?
             { bothering you?

Everybody says ...
People say ...
Everybody tells me ...
Most people say ...
I hear ...
They say ...

Conversation strategies

Hesitating

Hmm.
Well, ...
(Well,) let's see ...

Initiating a topic

You seem troubled/upset.
You don't seem to be yourself today.

Asking for repetition

Eh? What?
[more polite]
Sorry?
What?
Excuse me? } (Am.E.)
Pardon (me)?

Checking and indicating understanding

*Checking one's own
   understanding*

Tooth-brite?

130

UNIT 13: AGREEING AND DISAGREEING

Emphatic form, does/did, etc.
Tag questions
Might
Wouldn't you ...?
Present perfect
Present perfect continuous
Past continuous
Should (obligation)

13.1 Agreeing (1) 'I agree.'

(1) I agree (with you).
You're/That's right.
That's true.
I know.

(2) Absolutely!
Definitely!

A. We had a very good fourth quarter.
B. **I agree.**(1) We DID have a very good fourth quarter, didn't we?
A. **Absolutely!**(2)

1.

2.

3.

4.

5.

Now present your own conversations.

A. That was a terrible film!
B. It was.
A. I mean, the acting was awful . . .
B. **I agree.**(1)
A. . . . and the plot was impossible to follow.
B. **That's just what I was thinking.**(2)

(1) I agree.
You're right.
I know.

(2) That's just/exactly what I was thinking.
I couldn't agree with you more.
I feel the same way.
That's exactly what I think.
My feelings exactly.

[less formal]
You can say that again!
You took the words (right) out of my mouth!

She's an awful singer!
Her voice is so loud . . .
and she's singing out of tune.

1.

Mr and Mrs Wagner have such wonderful children.
They're very well-mannered . . .
and they're so friendly to everybody in the neighbourhood.

2.

This bus driver drives like a maniac!
He's constantly changing lanes . . .
and he's going much too fast.

3.

Walter made a fool of himself at the party!
He drank too much . . . and he told the same jokes he's been telling for years.

4.

Dr Frankenstein has been acting very strangely recently.
He's very nasty to everybody in the village . . . and I bet he's up to something in his laboratory.

5.

'THAT'S JUST WHAT I WAS THINKING.'

Now present your own conversations.

(1) That might/may be true.
You might/may be right.
You have a point (there).
I see your point.
I know.
Yes.

(2) But
However,

(3) wouldn't you agree (that)
wouldn't you say (that)
don't you think (that)

(4) I suppose you're right.
I suppose that's true.

A. This car is a very old model.
B. **That might be true.**(1) **But**(2) **wouldn't you agree that**(3) it's in excellent condition?
A. **I suppose you're right.**(4)

1.

2.

3.

4.

5.

'THAT MIGHT BE TRUE.'

Now present your own conversations.

13.4 Agreeing regretfully 'I'm afraid you're right.'

You've been very quiet recently.

A. You know, I've noticed that you've been very quiet recently.
B. **I'm afraid you're right.**[1] I HAVE been very quiet recently, haven't I.
A. **You have.**[2]

[1] I'm afraid you're right.
I'm afraid I have to agree.
I hate to admit/say it, but you're right.
I hate to admit/say it, but it's true.

[2] (You) have/haven't.
It's true.
No doubt about it!
Absolutely!
Definitely!

You've been gaining weight.

1.

You aren't as good-natured as you used to be.

2.

The grandchildren don't call as often as they used to.

3.

Your school work has been suffering since football practice started.

4.

Good old Rover isn't as young as he used to be.

5.

'I'M AFRAID YOU'RE RIGHT.'

Now present your own conversations.

135

13.5 Correcting politely 'That isn't exactly right.'

(1) Mr/Ms/Mrs/Miss _____
sir

(2) that isn't exactly/quite
right
that isn't exactly/quite
correct/true
I think you might be
mistaken

(3) Thank you for bringing
that to my attention.
Thank you for pointing
that out.
Thank you for correcting
me (on that). (Am.E.)

A. The bread goes in row four.
B. Excuse me, **Mr** Perkins,(1) but actually, **that isn't exactly right.**(2)
A. Oh?
B. Yes, Mr Perkins. Actually, the bread goes in row FIVE.
A. Oh. **Thank you for bringing that to my attention.**(3)

1. Excuse me, Mrs Alfredo . . .

2. Excuse me, sir . . .

3. Excuse me, Miss Whitehead . . .

4. Excuse me, Doctor . . .

5. Excuse me, Mr President . . .

Now present your own conversations.

13.6 Angry disagreement 'That's not true.'

(1) That's not true.
That's/You're wrong.
You're mistaken.
Certainly not.

(2) Come on!
Look!
Listen!

(3) Why don't you admit it?
You might as well own
up.
Admit it!

(4) I know
I'm sure
I'm convinced
I'm certain
I'm positive (Am.E.)

(5) I'm not (so) sure I believe
that.
I'm not so sure (about
that).

A. You've been reading my boyfriend's letters, haven't you.
B. **That's not true.**(1)
A. **Come on!**(2) **Why don't you admit it?**(3) **I know**(4) you
have.
B. That's just not true. I HAVEN'T been reading his letters!
A. Well, **I'm not so sure I believe that.**(5)

1.

2.

3.

4.

5.

Now present your own
conversations.

137

13.7 INTERCHANGE: Differences of opinion
'I'm not so sure about that.'

Somebody should do something about all the violence in children's cartoon programmes.

Kids aren't much affected by what they see on TV because they know it isn't real.

A. **Don't you think that**[1] somebody should do something about all the violence in children's cartoon programmes?
B. Well, **I'm not so sure about that.**[2]
A. Oh?
B. Yes. **I wish I could agree with you,**[3] but **if you ask me,**[4] kids aren't much affected by what they see on TV because they know it isn't real.
A. Well, **I disagree.**[5]

---

[1] Don't you think (that)
Wouldn't you say (that)
Wouldn't you agree that

[2] I'm not so sure (about that).
I don't know (about that).
I'm not sure (if) I agree (with you about that).
I wouldn't say that.
I wouldn't go as far as that.
I wouldn't go so far as to say that.

[3] I wish I could agree (with you).
I hate to disagree (with you)
I don't mean to disagree (with you)
I don't want to argue (with you) (about that)
I don't want to start/get into an argument (with you) (about it)

[4] if you ask me,
in my opinion,
as far as I'm concerned,
I personally think,
as I see it,
the way I see it,

[5] I disagree.
I don't agree.
I can't agree.
I don't think so.

You're having a disagreement with somebody. Create an original conversation using the model dialogue on p. 138 as a guide. Feel free to adapt and expand the model in any way you wish.

UNIT 13 SUMMARY

Functions

Agreement/Disagreement

Enquiring about . . .

Wouldn't you agree (that) _____?
Wouldn't you say (that) _____?
Don't you think (that) _____?

Expressing agreement

I agree (with you).
You're/That's right.
That's/It's true.
I know.

Absolutely!
Definitely!
No doubt about it!

That's just/exactly what I was
   thinking.
I couldn't agree with you more.
I feel the same way.
That's exactly what I think.
My feelings exactly.
[less formal]
You can say that again!
You took the words (right) out of my
   mouth!

I suppose you're right.
I suppose that's true.
That might/may be true.
You might/may be right.
You have a point (there).
I see your point.
I know.
Yes.

I'm afraid you're right.
I'm afraid I have to agree.
I hate to admit/say it, but you're
   right.
I hate to admit/say it, but it's true.

Expressing disagreement

I disagree.
I don't agree.
I can't agree.
I don't think so.

I'm not so sure (about that).
I don't know (about that).
I'm not sure (if) I agree (with you
   about that).
I wouldn't say that.
I wouldn't go as far as that.
I wouldn't go so far as to say that.

I wish I could agree (with you),
   but . . .
I hate to disagree (with you), but . . .
I don't mean to disagree (with you),
   but . . .
I don't want to argue (with you)
   (about that), but . . .
I don't want to start/get into an
   argument (with you) (about it),
   but . . .

(But/However,)
{ wouldn't you agree (that) _____?
{ wouldn't you say (that) _____?
{ don't you think (that) _____?

Correcting

Giving correction

That isn't exactly/quite right/correct/
   true.
I think you might be mistaken.
That's (just) not true!

(Actually,) *the bread goes in row FIVE.*

That's just not true! *I do like your cooking.*

Responding to correction

Thank you for bringing that to my
   attention.
Thank you for pointing that out.
Thank you for correcting me on that.
   (Am.E.)

Certainty/Uncertainty

Expressing . . .

I know _____.
I'm sure _____.
I'm convinced _____.
I'm certain _____.
I'm positive _____. (Am.E.)

I'm not so sure I believe that.
I'm not so sure (about that).

Denying/Admitting

Denying

That's not true.
That's/You're wrong.
You're mistaken.
That (just) isn't so.
Certainly not.

Asking for an admission

Why don't you admit it?
You might as well own up.
Admit it!

Persuading/Insisting

Come on!
Look!
Listen!

Conversation strategies

Initiating a topic

You know, . . .

Don't you think (that) _____?
Wouldn't you say (that) _____?
Wouldn't you agree (that) _____?

Focusing attention

If you ask me, . . .
In my opinion, . . .
As far as I'm concerned, . . .
I personally think . . .
As I see it, . . .
The way I see it . . .

140

UNIT 14: POSSIBILITY AND PROBABILITY

Short answers
Going to
Future (will)
Should (expectation)
Should have
Might
Might have
Must have (deduction)
Gerunds
Second conditional

14.1 Certainty 'Are you certain?'

(1) certain
sure
positive (Am.E.)

(2) I'm certain/sure/positive.
Absolutely!
Definitely!
Positively! (Am.E.)

(3) I definitely
There's no question (in my mind) I
I have no doubt (at all) (that) I

(4) There's no chance (that)
There's no possibility (that)

[less formal]
There's no way (that) (Am.E.)

A. Do you want to go through with this?
B. Yes, I do.
A. Are you **certain?**(1)
B. **I'm positive.**(2) I **definitely**(3) want to go through with this.

A. Is it going to rain?
B. No, it isn't.
A. Are you **sure?**(1)
B. **Absolutely!**(2) **There's no chance**(4) it's going to rain.

1. Do we have a test tomorrow?
   Yes ...

2. Will this hurt?
   No ...

3. Are you going to agree to the takeover?
   No ...

4. Are you capable of running our overseas operations?
   Yes ...

5. Did the butler do it?
   No ...

'ARE YOU CERTAIN...?'

Now present your own conversations

142

14.2 High probability 'That's most probably what I'll do.'

> What are you going to do next year?

A. What are you going to do next year?
B. **I'll probably**[1] *study law.*
A. Study law? Oh. Is that definite?
B. Well, I'm not **absolutely positive.**[2] But **that's most probably**[3] what I'll do.

[1] I'll probably
I'm pretty sure I'll
The chances are I'll
I'll most likely (Am.E.)

[2] absolutely sure/certain/
positive (about that)
a hundred per cent sure

[3] that's most probably
in all probability

> Where are you going to go for your holiday?

1. go on *a tour of the Greek islands*

> What are you going to call your new baby?

2. *Harry*

> When are you going to announce your retirement?

3. *at the next Board of Trustees meeting*

> How are you going to celebrate you birthday?

4. have *a party*

> What are you going to do with your prize money?

5. buy *a yacht*

'THAT'S MOST PROBABLY...?'

Now present your own conversations.

143

(1) It should
It ought to
It'll probably
In all probability it'll
The chances are it'll
It'll most likely (Am.E.)

A. When will the next bus from Brussels arrive?
B. **It should**(1) arrive any minute now.
A. Any minute now?
B. Yes, according to the timetable.

1. in half an hour
according to the recipe
on the box

2. within thirty days
according to company
policy

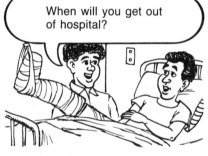

3. in four days
according to my doctor

4. seven working days
according to usual bank
procedures

5. Zurich
according to the flight
plan

Now present your own
conversations.

14.4 Conjecture 'She must have got stuck in the traffic.'

> **Our English teacher** should have arrived by now.

> She must have got stuck in the traffic.

A. I'm getting a little **worried**[1] about our English teacher. She should have arrived by now.
B. Oh, **I wouldn't worry.**[2] **She must have**[3] got stuck in the traffic.
A. I don't know. She **might have**[4] ... but then again, I'm not so sure. I'm afraid something must have happened.
B. Now **don't jump to conclusions.**[5] I'm sure she'll turn up for class soon.

[1] worried
     concerned
     anxious
     nervous

[2] I wouldn't worry.
     I wouldn't be concerned.
     Don't worry.
     Don't be concerned.
       (Am.E.)

[3] She must have
     She's probably
     She's most likely
     The chances are she's
     I wouldn't be surprised if
       she's
     [less formal]
     I/I'll bet she's

[4] might have
     may have

[5] Don't jump to conclusions.
     Don't get (yourself) (all)
       worked up.
     Don't get carried away.
     Don't let your imagination
       run away with you.

> **My wife's plane** should have landed by now.

> It must have been late taking off.

1.

> **My husband** should have been home by now.

> He must have got held up at the office.

2.

> **My daughter** should have been home from the party by 11 p.m.

> She must have lost track of the time.

3.

> **Our shipment of imported Christmas ornaments** should have been delivered by now.

> It must have been delayed by Customs.

4.

> **My request for a transfer** should have been approved by now.

> It must have got caught up in a lot of red tape.

5.

'SHE MUST HAVE...'

Now present your own conversations.

145

14.5 Possible courses of action 'I **might** buy the cheap one.'

(1) might
may

(2) On the other hand,
Then again,

(3) perhaps I'll
maybe I'll
I might
I may

(4) Take my advice!
Take it from me!
If you want my advice,

(5) be disappointed
be sorry
regret it

(6) I'll probably
I guess I'll
I suppose I'll

A.   Which model of washing machine are you interested in?
B.   I'm not sure. I **might**[1] buy the cheap one. **On the other hand,**[2] **perhaps I'll**[3] buy the deluxe model.
A.   **Take my advice!**[4] Don't buy the cheap one! You'll **be disappointed.**[5]
B.   Oh. Well, in that case, **I'll probably**[6] buy the deluxe model.
A.   You won't **be sorry.**[5]

1. see 'Moon over Manhattan'
see 'Dancers in Love'

2. take a bus tour
walk around on my own

3. ask for a small car
ask for a large car

4. take astronomy with
Professor Bright
take zoology with
Professor Hood

5. order the 'chicken
surprise'
order the 'beef Stroganoff'

Now present your own conversations.

14.6 Low probability
'There's not much chance of that happening.'

A. **What are the chances of**(1) my having twins?
B. **Probably not very high.**(2) **There's not much chance of that happening.**(3)
A. Oh? Are you absolutely sure about that?
B. Yes, I'm pretty certain. **In fact,**(4) if you had twins, I'd be very surprised.

(1) What are the chances of
What do you think the chances are of
What's the likelihood of
What's the possibility of
Is there much chance of

(2) Probably not very high/ great.
It/That isn't very likely.

[less formal]
Pretty slim.

(3) There's not much chance of that happening.
I doubt if that would/ could/will happen.
I don't think that will happen.
That's not likely to happen.
That's not very likely.

(4) In fact,
To tell the truth,

1.

3.

4.

5.

Now present your own conversations.

14.7 INTERCHANGE: Discussing possible decisions
'I don't know for sure.'

A. I've been meaning to ask you ... What are you going to do when our English course is finished?

B. I don't know. I think I might enrol in a more advanced class.

A. Oh. Is there much chance of your doing that?

B. Perhaps, but I don't know for sure. If I don't enrol in a more advanced class, maybe I'll take private lessons. What do you think?

A. How do you mean?

B. What do you think I should do? Any ideas?

A. Hmm. Well, I don't know ... er ... I suppose if I had to choose between enrolling in a more advanced class and taking private lessons, I'd probably enrol in a more advanced class. But of course that's only my opinion.

B. That's interesting. Why would you do that?

A. Well ... because there's an advantage in studying in a group and being able to practise speaking with lots of other students.

B. Hmm. That makes sense. I'll bear that in mind when I finally make my decision. And how about YOU?

A. Me?

B. Yes. What are YOU going to do when our English course is finished?

A. I've been meaning to ask you ... What are you going to do _____?

B. I don't know. I think I might _____.

A. Oh. Is there much chance of your doing that?

B. Perhaps, but I don't know for sure. If I don't _____, maybe I'll _____. What do you think?

A. How do you mean?

B. What do you think I should do? Any ideas?

A. Hmm ... Well, I don't know ... er ... I suppose if I had to choose between _____ing and _____ing, I'd probably _____. But of course that's only my opinion.

B. That's interesting. Why would you do that?

A. Well ... because _____.

B. Hmm. That makes sense. I'll bear that in mind when I finally make my decision. And how about YOU?

A. Me?

B. Yes. What are YOU going to do _____?

A. ....

You're discussing future plans (about work, school, personal matters, etc.) with a friend. Create an original conversation using the model dialogue above as a guide, and using functional expressions found throughout this unit. Feel free to adapt and expand the model in any way you wish.

UNIT 14 SUMMARY

Functions

Probability/Improbability

Enquiring about ...

What are the chances of _____?
What do you think the chances are of _____?
What's the likelihood of _____?
What's the possibility of _____?
Is there much/a good chance _____?

Expressing ...

I'll probably _____.
I'm pretty sure I'll _____.
The chances are I'll _____.
I guess I'll _____.
I suppose I'll _____.
I'll most likely _____. (Am.E.)

That's most probably ...
In all probability ...

If I had to choose between _____ and _____, I'd probably _____.

It should
It ought to
It'll probably
In all probability it'll
The chances are it'll
It'll most likely
  (Am.E.)
} *arrive any minute now.*

The chances are probably not very high.
It/That isn't very likely.
[less formal]
The chances are pretty slim.

There's not much chance of that happening.
I doubt if that would/could/will happen.
I don't think that will happen.
That's not likely to happen.
That's not very likely.

Fear/Worry/Anxiety

I'm (getting) (a little) {worried / concerned / anxious / nervous} {about _____,}

I'm afraid something must have happened (to him/her/them/it).

I wouldn't worry.
I wouldn't be concerned.
Don't worry.
Don't be concerned. (Am.E.)

Warning

You'll be disappointed.
You'll be sorry.
You'll regret it.

Possibility/Impossibility

Enquiring about ...

What's the possibility of _____?

Expressing possibility

I might _____.
I may _____.
Perhaps I'll _____.
Maybe I'll _____.

Perhaps.

_____ might have _____ed.
_____ may have _____ed.

Expressing impossibility

There's no chance (that) _____.
There's no possibility (that) _____.
[less formal]
There's no way (that) _____. (Am.E.)

Certainty/Uncertainty

Enquiring about ...

Are you certain/sure/positive?

Are you (absolutely) sure about that?

Is that definite?

Expressing ...

I'm (absolutely) certain/sure/positive (that _____).
Absolutely!
Definitely!
Positively! (Am.E.)

I definitely _____.
There's no question (in my mind) _____.

I have no doubt (at all) (that) _____.

I'm pretty certain.

I'm not absolutely sure/certain/positive (about that).
I'm not a hundred percent sure.

I'm not (so) sure.
I don't know for sure.

Advice/Suggestions

Asking for ...

What do you think (I should do)?
Any ideas?

Offering ...

Take my advice!
Take it from me!
If you want my advice,

Don't jump to conclusions.
Don't get (yourself) all worked up.
Don't get carried away.
Don't let your imagination run away with you.

There's an advantage in _____ing.

Deduction

_____ should have _____ed (by now).

_____ must have _____.
_____ probably _____.
_____ most likely _____.
The chances are _____.
I wouldn't be surprised if _____.
[less formal]
I/I'll bet _____.

Intention

Enquiring about ...

What are you going to do (*next year*)?

Conversation strategies

Initiating a topic

I've been meaning to ask you ...

Focusing attention

In fact, ...
To tell the truth, ...

Hesitating

Hmm.
Well, ...
Well, I don't know ...
Er ...

Checking and indicating understanding

Checking one's own understanding

Any minute now?

SCENES AND IMPROVISATIONS
Units 12–14

Who do you think these people are?
What do you think they're talking about?
Create conversations based on these scenes and act them out.

1.

2.

3.

4.

5.

6.

7.

8.

UNIT 15: WISHING AND REGRETTING

15.1 *Regretting (1)*
'It's a shame this restaurant is so expensive.'

15.2 *Wishing (1)*
'I wish we had a newer car.'

15.3 *Wishing (2)*
'If only I could communicate with my boss.'

15.4 *Regretting (2)*
'I've been very stupid.'

15.5 *Regretting (3)*
'I regret having to fire Mr Smith.'

15.6 *Interchange: Regretting (4)*
'I'm sorry I didn't start English lessons when I was young.'

Summary

Wish clauses
2nd conditional
3rd conditional
If only . . .
Gerunds

(1) It's a shame (that)
It's a pity (that)
I'm disappointed (that)
It's disappointing (that)
(It's) too bad (that)
(Am.E.)

(2) I agree (with you).
You're/That's right.
That's true.
I know.

(3) So do I.
Me, too.
I think so, too.
I feel the same way.
I do too.

(4) seems (as if/as though)
appears (as if/as though)
looks like (Am.E.)

This restaurant is so **expensive** . . . we can't eat here tonight.

A. **It's a shame**(1) this restaurant is so expensive.
B. **I agree.**(2) I wish it were cheaper.
A. **So do I.**(3) I was hoping we could eat here tonight, but it **seems**(4) that's out of the question.
B. I'm afraid so.

The weather is so **bad** . . . we can't go to the beach.

1.

This machine is so **slow** . . . we won't be able to finish copying this report today.

2.

The boss is in such a **bad** mood . . . I can't ask him to give me tomorrow off.

3.

The union's wage demands are so **high** . . . we won't be able to negotiate an agreement by midnight.

4.

These instructions are so **complicated** . . . we won't be able to put this bicycle together for Pat's birthday.

5.

'IT'S A SHAME...'

Now present your own conversations.

15.2 Wishing (1) 'I wish we had a newer car.'

A. You know what I wish?
B. What?
A. I wish we had a newer car.
B. I know. **It's a shame**[1] we don't. If we had a newer car, we wouldn't spend so much money on repairs.
A. **That's exactly what I was thinking.**[2]

[1] It's a shame (that)
It's a pity (that)
It's too bad (that) (Am.E.)

[2] That's (exactly/just) what I was thinking.
That's (exactly) what I think.

[less formal]
You can say that again!
You took the words (right) out of my mouth!
You're (so/too) right.

Now present your own conversations.

(1) I've been meaning
I keep forgetting
I keep meaning

(2) Do you really want to know?
Do you want to know the truth?

(3) the truth is
the fact of the matter is

(4) That's a shame/a pity.
What a shame/a pity.
That's too bad. (Am.E.)

(5) If only I could
I wish I could

(6) It's not that easy/simple.
It's easier said than done.
It's not as easy/simple as that.

A. **I've been meaning**(1) to ask you . . . How are you enjoying your new job?
B. **Do you really want to know?**(2)
A. Yes.
B. Well, **the truth is,**(3) I'm not enjoying my new job at all.
A. **That's too bad.**(4) I'm sorry to hear that.
B. **If only I could**(5) communicate with my boss.
A. Why can't you?
B. **It's not that easy.**(6) Communicating with my boss is very difficult.
A. I'm sure it is. But don't give up trying.
B. Oh, don't worry. I won't.

1.   2.

Now present your own conversations.

(1) I could kick myself!
I'm an idiot/a fool!

[stronger]
I could shoot myself!
(Am.E.)

(2) I've been very stupid/
foolish.
I've made a dreadful/
awful/terrible mistake.

[less formal]
I (have) (really) goofed!
(Am.E.)

(3) Do you mean (to say)
Are you saying
Are you telling me
Does that mean

(4) It's all my fault.
I'm (entirely) to blame.
It's all my doing.

(5) That's terrible!
That's awful!
That's dreadful!
That's too bad! (Am.E.)

A. **I could kick myself!**(1)
B. Why?
A. **I've been very stupid.**(2) I forgot to fill up the tank before we left.
B. Oh! **Do you mean to say**(3) we've run out of petrol?
A. I'm afraid we have and **it's all my fault.**(4) If I hadn't forgotten to fill up the tank before we left, we wouldn't have run out of petrol. I wish I hadn't been so stupid!
B. **That's terrible!**(5)

1.

2.

Now present your own conversations.

15.5 Regretting (3) 'I regret having to fire Mr Smith.'

(1) I regret _____ing.
I regret (that) I _____.
I'm sorry about _____ing.
I'm sorry (that) I _____.

(2) choice
alternative
other option
other recourse (Am.E.)

(3) Perhaps
Apparently
Evidently
Obviously

(4) I wasn't aware of that.
I didn't know that.

(5) How awful/dreadful/
terrible!
That's too bad! (Am.E.)

(6) under the circumstances
given the circumstances
given the situation

I have to fire Mr Smith. He embezzled company funds.

A. You know, **I regret**(1) having to fire Mr Smith.
B. Well then, why are you going to do it?
A. I've got no **choice.**(2) **Perhaps**(3) you're not aware that he embezzled company funds.
B. Oh no! **I wasn't aware of that.**(4) **How awful!**(5)
A. Yes, it really is. If he hadn't embezzled company funds, I wouldn't have made this decision.
B. Well, **under the circumstances,**(6) I can see why you're doing it.

I'm forced to close down the business.
The new shopping centre has taken all my customers away.

1.

I have to give up driving for a while.
My doctor said I needed a complete rest.

2.

I'm obliged to evict you from your flat.
The building has been sold to developers.

3.

I'm forced to break up with my boyfriend.
He's got a drinking problem.

4.

I'm making Johnny repeat a year.
He has not kept up with his classmates.

5.

'I REGRET...'

Now present your own conversations.

15.6 INTERCHANGE: Regretting (4)
'I'm sorry I didn't start English lessons when I was young.'

A. You know, I've been thinking.
B. What?
A. I'm sorry I didn't start English lessons when I was young.
B. Really?
A. Yes. I wish I'd begun when I was five or so.
B. Hmm. What makes you say that?
A. Well, if I'd started learning English when I was very young, I wouldn't be having so much trouble with the pronunciation.
B. Yes, **I do see what you mean.**[1]

A. You know, I've been thinking.
B. What?
A. I regret being so shy.
B. Really?
A. Yes. I wish I felt more comfortable in a large group of people.
B. Hmm. What makes you say that?
A. Well, if I weren't so shy, I wouldn't feel so uneasy at parties.
B. Yes, **I do see what you mean.**[1]

---

[1] I (do) see what you mean.
I can understand (why you feel that way).

A. You know, I've been thinking.
B. What?
A. I'm sorry/I regret _____.
B. Really?
A. Yes. I wish_____.
B. Hmm. What makes you say that?
A. Well, if _____.
B. Yes, I do see what you mean.

You've been thinking about something you regret. Create an original conversation using the model dialogue above as a guide and using functional expressions found throughout this unit. Feel free to adapt and expand the model in any way you wish.

UNIT 15 SUMMARY

Functions

Regret

It's a shame (that) _____.
It's a pity (that) _____.
I'm disappointed (that) _____.
It's disappointing (that) _____.
(It's) too bad (that) _____. (Am.E.)

I regret _____ing.
I regret (that) I _____.
I'm sorry about _____ing.
I'm sorry (that) I _____.

I could kick myself!
I'm an idiot/a fool!
[stronger]
I could shoot myself! (Am.E.)

Agreement/Disagreement

Expressing agreement

I agree (with you).
You're/That's right.
That's true.
I know.

That's (exactly/just) what I was
   thinking.
That's (exactly) what I think.
[less formal]
You can say that again!
You took the words (right) out of
   my mouth!
You're (so/too) right.

So do I.
Me, too.
I think so, too.
I feel the same way.
I do too.

Under the circumstances, I can see
_____.
Given the circumstances, I can see
_____.
Given the situation, I can see _____.

Wish/Hope

I wish *it were cheaper.*

I wish I could _____.
If only I could _____.

I was hoping _____.

Denying/Admitting

Admitting

The truth is . . .
The fact of the matter is . . .

I've been very stupid/foolish.
I've made a dreadful/awful/terrible
   mistake.
[less formal]
I (have) (really) goofed! (Am.E.)

It's all my fault.
I'm (entirely) to blame.
It's all my doing.

Satisfaction/Dissatisfaction

Enquiring about . . .

How are you enjoying _____?

Expressing dissatisfaction

I'm not enjoying _____ (at all).

Sympathizing

That's a shame/a pity.
What a shame/a pity.
That's terrible/awful/dreadful.
How awful/dreadful/terrible!
I'm sorry to hear that.
That's too bad. (Am.E.)

Remembering/Forgetting

Indicating . . .

I forgot to _____.
I've been meaning to _____.

Asking for and reporting
information

What makes you say that?

Perhaps
Apparently } you're not aware that
Evidently } _____.
Obviously

Conversation strategies

Initiating a topic

You know *what I wish?*

I've been meaning to ask you . . .
I keep forgetting to ask you . . .
I keep meaning to ask you . . .

(You know,) I've been thinking . . .

Clarification

Asking for clarification

Do you mean (to say) _____?
Are you saying _____?
Does that mean _____?

UNIT 16: MISCELLANEOUS

16.1 *Apologizing*
'I'm sorry I'm late.'

16.2 *Criticizing*
'I (do) wish you hadn't had the coffee machine removed.'

16.3 *Requesting clarification* (1)
'I'm afraid I don't follow you.'

16.4 *Interrupting*
'Oh, by the way, the new photocopier arrived this morning.'

16.5 *Requesting clarification* (2)
'I'm sorry, I didn't hear what you said.'

16.6 *Expressing ability*
'I've had a lot of experience taking shorthand.'

16.7 *Expressing obligations* (1)
'You're supposed to have your request approved.'

16.8 *Interchange: Expressing obligations* (2)
'Let me tell you about some of our policies and practices.'

Summary

Gerunds
Present perfect (+ 'ever')
Wish (someone) had (not) done something
3rd conditional
Imperatives
Question forms
To have (something) done
To want (someone) to do (something)

16.1 Apologizing 'I'm sorry I'm late.'

(1) I'm sorry I _____.
(I'm) sorry for _____ing.
I apologize for _____ing.
Forgive me for _____ing.
I'd like to apologize for _____ing.

(2) That's/It's okay.
That's/It's all right.
That/It doesn't matter.

(3) I'm really/very sorry.
I feel terrible/bad.

(4) Don't worry about it.
These things (will/do) happen.
[informal]
No problem.
Not to worry.

A. **I'm sorry I**(1)**'m late.**
B. **That's okay.**(2)
A. You know, this is the first time I've ever been late. **I'm really sorry.**(3)
B. **Don't worry about it.**(4)

1. forget our anniversary

2. fall asleep in class

3. shout at you

4. come back late from lunch

5. not remember my lines

Now present your own conversations.

16.2 Criticizing 'I (do) wish you hadn't had the coffee machine removed.'

The office staff are all fed up!

A. You know ... I hate to say this ... but I do wish you hadn't had the coffee machine removed.
B. Really? **Why do you say that?**[1] **What's the matter?**[2]
A. Don't you realize that **as a result of**[3] what you did, the office staff are all fed up?!
B. I'm sorry. **I hadn't thought of that.**[4] If I'd **known**[5] the office staff were going to be all fed up, I wouldn't have had the coffee machine removed. **I apologize.**[6]

[1] Why do you say that?
    What makes you say that?

[2] What's the matter?
    What's wrong?
    What's the problem?

[3] as a result of
    because of

[4] I hadn't thought of that.
    That hadn't occurred to me.
    That never entered my head.

[5] known
    realized

[6] I apologize.
    I'm sorry.
    (Please) forgive me.
    Please accept my apologies.

I'm not going to sleep a wink until he gets home!

1. let Peter have the car tonight

I'm getting heartburn!

2. ask for garlic and pepperoni on this pizza

We might not have enough money to pay the heating bills!

3. promise the kids new bicycles for Christmas

I'm the laughing stock of the whole school!

4. make me get such a short haircut

He's probably going to raise our quota!

5. tell the foreman how fast we can produce these teddy bears

'I (DO) WISH YOU HADN'T...'

Now present your own conversations.

16.3 Requesting clarification (1)
'I'm afraid I don't follow you.'

(1) [less direct]
I'm afraid I don't follow you.
I'm not (really) sure what
   you're getting at.
I'm afraid I'm not with you.
I'm not quite clear (as to)
   what you mean (by that).
I'm afraid I'm not
   following you. (Am.E.)

[more direct]
What do you mean (by that)?
What does that mean?

(2) Let me put it this way:
Let me put it another way:
What I'm (really) saying is
What I'm trying to say is
What I mean is
What I'm getting at is
In other words

(3) I understand.
I follow you.
I see.

[informal]
I get you/it.

A. The X-rays suggest that an extraction is indicated.
B. **I'm afraid I don't follow you.**(1)
A. Okay. **Let me put it this way:**(2) I'm going to have to pull your tooth out.
B. Oh, now **I understand.**(3)

1. 'The war ended.'

2. 'You're fired.'

3. 'I think we should break up.'

4. 'The bookkeeper is going to leave.'

5. 'I'm going to have a baby.'

Now present your own conversations.

16.4 Interrupting 'Oh, by the way, the new photocopier arrived this morning.'

A. Now, **regarding**[(1)] the merger with the Commercial Bank, . . .
B. **Oh, by the way,**[(2)] the new photocopier arrived this morning.
A. Oh, I didn't know that. Now, **as I was saying,**[(3)] regarding the merger with the Commercial Bank, **in my opinion,**[(4)] . . .
B. Excuse me for interrupting, but I'm afraid it's getting late. **I've really got to go now.**[(5)]
A. Oh. That's too bad. We haven't really had a chance to talk about the merger with . . .
B. I know. I'm sorry. Let's continue the conversation soon.

(1) regarding _____,
regarding the issue of _____,
as far as _____ is
   concerned, about,

(2) (Oh,) by the way/bye,
(Oh,) incidentally,
(Oh,) before I forget,
I don't mean to change
   the subject, but

(3) as I was saying,
to get back to what I was
   saying,
to get back to what we
   were talking about,

(4) in my opinion,
as I see it,
the way I see it,
if you ask me,
the thing to keep in mind is

(5) I've (really) got to go (now).
I've (really) got to be
   going (now).
I (really) must go (now).
I (really) must be going
   (now).
I (really) have to go (now).
I'd (really) better go (now).
I (really) should go (now).
I have to/I've got to run.
I have to/I've got to get
   going.

1.

3.

4.

5.

Now present your own conversations.

16.5 Requesting clarification (2)
'I'm sorry, I didn't hear what you said.'

(1) I didn't hear what you said.
  I didn't hear you.
  I didn't catch what you said.
  I didn't quite catch that.
  What did you say?
  I beg your pardon.
  Pardon me. (Am.E.)

(2) WHEN do you want me to
  WHEN should I
  WHEN did you tell me to

A. Please report for work tomorrow at 7:45.
B. I'm sorry, **I didn't hear what you said.**(1)
   WHEN do you want me to(2) report for work tomorrow?
A. At 7:45.
B. Oh, okay.

1. Please give these packages to Tom.

2. Please get a loaf of bread and a dozen eggs at the supermarket.

3. Put three slices of tomato on each salad.

4. Take these pills four times a day.

5. Put the money in a brown paper bag.

'I'M SORRY I DIDN'T HEAR WHAT YOU SAID'

Now present your own conversations.

16.6 Expressing ability
'I've had a lot of experience taking shorthand.'

A. **Can you**[1] take shorthand?
B. Yes, I can. **I've had a lot of experience**[2] taking shorthand.
A. Then you'd **consider yourself**[3] an **experienced**[4] stenographer?
B. **Yes, I would.**[5]

[1] Can you
    Are you able to
    Do you know how to

[2] I've had a lot of experience
    I'm very good at

[3] consider yourself
    say you were

[4] experienced
    capable

[5] Yes, I would.
    I would say so.

1. type technical reports
    typist

2. repair foreign cars
    mechanic

3. operate a computer
    data processor

4. fix window frames and doors
    carpenter

5. perform this operation
    surgeon

Now present your own
conversations.

16.7 Expressing obligation
'You're supposed to have your request approved.'

(1) submit
put in
hand in
give you
turn in (Am.E.)

(2) You're supposed to
You're required to
You're expected to
You need to
You have to
You've got to
You must
It's necessary (for you) to
It's required that you
   (Am.E.)

(3) processed
accepted
considered
reviewed
evaluated
acted upon
taken into consideration

(4) required
necessary
essential
obligatory
compulsory
mandatory (Am.E.)

A. I'd like to **submit**(1) my request for maternity leave.
B. Have you had it approved by your supervisor?
A. Excuse me. Have I had it what?!
B. Approved by your supervisor. **You're supposed to**(2) have your request for maternity leave approved by your supervisor before it can be **processed.**(3)
A. Oh. I haven't done that. I didn't know that was **required.**(4)
B. Oh, yes. It's **essential.**(4)

1. signed by your parents

2. signature witnessed

3. checked by one of our secretaries

4. signed by your doctor

5. signed by your spouse

Now present your own conversations.

16.8 INTERCHANGE: Expressing obligations (2)
'Let me tell you about some of our policies and practices.'

A. **Let me tell you about**[1] some of our policies and practices here at Anchor Insurance.
B. Please do.
A. **We expect all our employees to**[2] arrive **on time**[3] in the morning, and we insist that they keep their lunch hours to a reasonable length.
B. I quite understand.
A. Good character is very important to us. We require all our staff here at Anchor Insurance to be industrious, co-operative and honest.
B. I'm glad to hear that.
A. And for our part, we try to do the best we can for our employees. **We feel obliged to**[4] provide a safe and pleasant work environment and **we make every effort to**[5] listen to our employees and meet their requests.
B. That sounds admirable.
A. Now, perhaps you have some questions to put to me. Is there any additional information you'd like me to give you?
B. Yes, as a matter of fact I do have a few questions.
A. Please go ahead.
B. Could you tell me whether a medical examination is **compulsory**[6] before one joins the firm?
A. Yes, it is.
B. And would I have to undergo any special training?
A. Yes, definitely.
B. Would it be necessary for me to work at weekends?
A. That wouldn't be necessary.
B. And one more question: do your employees have to serve a probation period before being given a permanent contract?
A. No, they don't.
B. I see.
   [Silent pause]
B. Well, **I've probably taken up enough of your time.**[7] I'll look forward to hearing from you when my application has been considered.
A. We'll be in touch with you shortly.
B. **I've enjoyed our talk.**[8] Thank you very much.
A. **It's been a pleasure.**[9]

(1) Let me tell you about
Let me explain

(2) We expect all our employees to _____.
We require all our employees to _____.
We insist that all our employees _____.

(3) on time
punctually

(4) We feel obliged to _____.
We feel compelled to _____.
We feel we must _____.
We feel we have to _____.
We feel we should _____.

(5) We make every effort to _____.
We do our best to _____.
We try our hardest to _____.

(6) compulsory
necessary
obligatory
required

(7) I've probably taken up enough of your time.
I know you're a very busy person.
I don't want to waste any more of your time.

(8) I've enjoyed our talk.
It's been a pleasant interview.
It's been a pleasure talking to you.
I've enjoyed talking with you. (Am.E.)

(9) It's been a pleasure.
It's been my pleasure.
(Please) don't mention it.
You're welcome. (Am.E.)

A. **Let me tell you about**[1] some of our policies and practices _____.
B. Please do.
A. **We expect all our employees to**[2] _____, and we insist that they _____.
B. I quite understand.
A. _____ is very important to us. We require all our staff here at _____ _____ to be _____.
B. I'm glad to hear that.
A. And for our part we try to _____ our employees. **We feel obliged to**[4] _____ and **we make every effort to**[5] _____.
B. That sounds _____.
A. Now, perhaps you have some questions to put to me. Is there any additional information you'd like me to give you?
B. Yes, as a matter of fact I do have a few questions.
A. Please go ahead.
B. Could you tell me whether _____ is **compulsory**[6] before one joins the firm?
A. Yes, it is.
B. And would I have to _____?
A. Yes, definitely.
B Would it be necessary for me to _____?
A. That wouldn't be necessary.
B. And one more question: _____?
A. _____.
B. I see.
A. [Silent pause]
B. Well, **I've probably taken up enough of your time.**[7] I'll look forward to hearing from you when my application has been considered.
A. We'll be in touch with you shortly.
B. **I've enjoyed our talk.**[8] Thank you very much.
A. **It's been a pleasure.**[9]

You have put in an application for a job and have been called for an interview. Create an original conversation using the model dialogue above as a guide. Feel free to adapt and expand the model in any way you wish.

UNIT 16 SUMMARY

Functions

Apologizing

Offering . . .

(I'm) sorry
I apologize
Forgive me
I'd like to apologize
} for _____ing.

I'm sorry I _____.

I'm (really/very) sorry.
I feel terrible/bad.

I apologize.
I'm sorry.
Please forgive me.
Please accept my apologies.

Accepting . . .

That's/It's okay.
That's/It's all right.
That/It doesn't matter.
Don't worry about it.
These things (will/do) happen.
[informal]
No problem.
Not to worry.

Criticizing

I (do) wish you had (not) _____ed.
As a result of what you _____ed . . .

Leave taking

I've (really) got to go (now).
I've (really) got to be going (now).
I (really) must go (now).
I (really) must be going (now).
I (really) have to go (now).
I'd (really) better go (now).
I (really) should go (now).
I have to run.
I have to get going.
I've got to run.
I've got to get going.
(Well,) I've probably taken up enough of your time.
(Well,) I know you're a very busy person.
(Well,) I don't want to waste any more of your time.

I've enjoyed our talk.
It's been a pleasant interview.
It's been a pleasure talking to you.
I've enjoyed talking with you. (Am.E.)

Obligation

Expressing . . .

It's required/necessary/essential/mandatory. (Am.E.)

You're supposed to _____.
You're required to _____.
You're expected to _____.
You need to _____.
You have to _____.
You've got to _____.
You must _____.
It's necessary (for you) to _____.
It's required that you _____. (Am.E.)

I didn't know that was required/obligatory/compulsory/necessary/essential/mandatory. (Am.E.)

We feel obligated to _____.
We feel compelled to _____.
We feel we must _____.
We feel we have to _____.
We feel we should . . . .

Ability/Inability

Enquiring about . . .

Can you _____?
Are you able to _____?
Do you know how to _____?

You'd consider yourself an experienced/capable _____?
You'd say you're an experienced/capable _____?

Expressing ability

I can (_____).

I'm very good at _____ing.

I've had a lot of experience _____ing.

Asking for and reporting information

Why do you say that?
What makes you say that?

What's the matter?
What's wrong?
What's the problem?

Conversation strategies

Clarification

Asking for clarification

[less direct]
I'm afraid I don't follow you.
I'm not (really) sure what you're getting at.
I'm afraid I'm not with you.
I'm not quite clear (as to) what you mean (by that).
I'm afraid I'm not following you. (Am.E.)
[more direct]
What do you mean (by that)?
What does that mean?

Giving clarification

Let me put it this way: ...
Let me put it another way: ...
What I'm (really) saying is ...
What I'm trying to say is ...
What I mean is ...
What I'm getting at is ...
In other words ... .

Checking and indicating understanding

Indicating understanding

(Now) { I understand.
       { I follow you.
       { I see.
[informal]
I get you/it.

Directing/Redirecting a conversation

(Oh,) by the way/bye, ...
(Oh,) incidentally, ...
(Oh,) before I forget, ...
I don't mean to change the subject, but ...

(Now) as I was saying, ...
(Now) to get back to what I was saying, ...
(Now) to get back to what we were talking about, ...

Focusing attention

In my opinion, ...
As I see it, ...
The way I see it, ...
If you ask me, ...
The thing to keep in mind is ...

Initiating a topic

Let me tell you about _____.
Let me explain _____.
(Now,) regarding _____, ...
(Now,) regarding the issue of _____, ...
(Now,) as far as _____ is concerned, ...

You know, ...

I hate to say this ... but ...

Asking for repetition

I didn't hear what you said.
I didn't hear you.
I didn't catch what you said.
I didn't quite catch that.
What did you say?
I beg your pardon.
Pardon me. (Am.E.)

WHEN do you want me to _____?
WHEN should I _____?
WHEN did you tell me to _____?

Excuse me.

Have I had it what?!

Interrupting

Excuse me for interrupting, (but) ...

SCENES AND IMPROVISATIONS
Units 15—16

Who do you think these people are?
What do you think they're talking about?
Create conversations based on these scenes and act them out.

1.

2.

3.

4.

5.

6.

7.

8.

APPENDIX: INVENTORY OF FUNCTIONS AND CONVERSATION STRATEGIES

Note References are to lesson units not page numbers.

Functions

Ability/Inability

Enquiring about . . .

Can you _____?
Are you able to _____?
Do you know how to _____?   16

Can you _____?
Is there any chance you could
   (possibly) _____?
Would you be able to _____?   10

You'd consider yourself an
   experienced/capable _____?
You'd say you're an experienced/
   capable _____?   16

Expressing ability

I can (_____).   16

I'm (very) good at _____ing.   16

I've had a lot of experience
   _____ing.   16

Expressing inability

I can't _____.
I won't be able to _____.
I'm not going to be able to
   _____.   7,10

I wasn't able to _____.
I couldn't _____.   6

I'm not sure (that) I can.   10

I can't make it on _____.
I'm tied up on _____.   10

I'd like to/love to, but I'm afraid I
   can't.   11

I'd do so willingly, but I'm afraid I
   can't.   11

There's nothing I can do about it.
There's no way I can get out of it.
I can't get out of it.   7

Advice/Suggestions

Asking for . . .

What do you think (I should do)?
Any ideas?   14

Any other suggestions?   12

Do you have any suggestions/
   recommendations/ideas/
   thoughts?   12

What do you suggest/recommend?   12

Can you recommend _____?
I was wondering if you could
   recommend _____.   12

I need your advice.   12

Offering . . .

Can I offer you some advice?
Can I give you a piece of advice?
Can I make a suggestion?   12

I (strongly) advise you to _____.
I urge you to _____.
I recommend that you _____.
I recommend _____ing.   12

You should (definitely) _____.
You ought to _____.
You must _____.
You'd better _____.
Be sure to _____.   12,14

You should _____.
Why don't you _____?
How about _____ing?   3

I think you should/ought to _____.
I/I'd suggest that you _____.
I/I'd suggest _____ing.
If I were you, I'd _____.
It seems to me (that) you should
   _____.
Don't you think you should _____?
Don't you think it would/might be a
   good idea to _____?
Be sure to _____.   12

Maybe you ought to/should _____.
Maybe you should consider _____ing.
It might be a good idea to _____.
Why don't you _____?   4

Have you considered _____ing?
Have you thought of _____ing?
Have you thought about _____ing?
You might consider _____ing.
Why don't you _____?
You could (always) _____.
How about _____ing?
What about _____ing?
It might be a good idea to _____.
What if you were to _____?   12

How about _____ing?
What about _____ing?
I/I'd suggest _____.
I/I'd recommend _____.   12

How about _____ing?
What about _____ing?
Let's _____.
What if we _____ed?
Why don't we _____?
We could (always) _____.
Would you be interested in
   _____(ing)?   4,12

Maybe we should _____.
Maybe we shouldn't _____.   4

They say that _____ is very good.
One of my favourite _____s is
   _____.   4

Is _____ okay?   4

There's an advantage in _____ing.   14

Take my advice!
Take it from me!
If you want my advice, _____.   14

Don't jump to conclusions!
Don't get (yourself) (all) worked up.
Don't get carried away.
Don't let your imagination run away
   with you.   14

Responding to . . .

(That's a/What a) good idea.
(That's a/What a) good suggestion.
That sounds good/great.
That sounds like a good idea.   12

I hadn't thought of that.
That hadn't occurred to me.   12

That never entered my mind.   12

Agreement/Disagreement

Enquiring about . . .

Wouldn't you agree (that) _____?
Wouldn't you say (that) _____?
Don't you think (that) _____?   13

Expressing agreement

I agree (with you).
You're/That's right.
That's/It's true.
I know.
[less formal]
You can say that again!
I'll say! (Am.E.)   7,13,15

Absolutely!
Definitely!
No doubt about it!   13

So do I.
Me, too.
I think so, too.
I feel the same way.
I do too.   15

That's (just/exactly) what I was
   thinking.
I couldn't agree with you more.
I feel the same way.
That's (exactly) what I think.

177

My feelings exactly.
[less formal]
You can say that again!
You took the words (right) out of
  my mouth!   13,15
You're (so/too) right.   15

I suppose you're right.
I suppose that's true.
That might/may be true.
You might/may be right.
You have a point (there).
I see your point.
I know.
Yes.   13

I'm afraid you're right.
I'm afraid I have to agree.
I hate to admit/say it, but you're
  right.
I hate to admit/say it, but it's true. 13

Under the circumstances, I can see
  _____.
Given the circumstances, I can see
  _____.
Given the situation, I can see
  _____.   15

Expressing disagreement

I disagree.
I don't agree.
I can't agree.
I don't think so.   13

I wish I could agree (with you),
  but . . .
I hate to disagree (with you), but . . .
I don't mean to disagree (with you),
  but . . .
I don't want to argue (with you)
  (about that), but . . .
I don't want to start/get into an
  argument (with you) (about it),
  but . . .   13

I'm not so sure (about that).
I don't know (about that).
I'm not sure (if) I agree (with you
  about that).
I wouldn't say that.
I wouldn't go as far as that.
I wouldn't go so far as to say
  that.   13

(But/However,)
{ wouldn't you agree (that) _____?
{ wouldn't you say (that) _____?
{ don't you think (that) _____?   13

Apologizing

Offering . . .

I'm sorry.
Excuse me. (Am.E.)   1

(Oh,) I'm sorry.   9

I apologize.
I'm sorry.
Please forgive me.
Please accept my apologies.   16

(I'm) sorry
I apologize
Forgive me   for _____ing.
I'd like to
  apologize.   16

I'm sorry I _____.   16

I'm (really/very/awfully) sorry.
I feel terrible/bad.   11,16

I don't mean to { make things difficult/
                 complicated for you.
                { complicate things.
                { give you a hard
                  time.   9

Accepting . . .

That's/It's all right.
Don't worry about it.
These things (will/do) happen.
[informal]
No problem.
Not to worry.   16

Appreciation

It's very good of you.
It's nice/kind of you to offer.
Thanks for offering.
I appreciate your offering.
That's (very) nice/kind of you.
That would be nice.
I appreciate it/that. }
I'd appreciate it/that. } (Am.E.)   8

I really appreciate it.
I appreciate it very much.   8,11

It was very nice of you (to _____).   8

I want to express my appreciation/
  gratitude to _____.   8

I can't begin to tell you how much I
  appreciate _____.   8

You're very kind/nice.   8

Asking for and reporting information

Where are you from?
  Japan.
What do you do?
  I'm an *English teacher.*
Which *flat do you live in?*
How long *have you been studying here?*
Who *is your doctor?*
Whose *family do you belong to?*
What kind of *music do you play?*
When *are you due?*   1

How about you?
What about you?
And you?   1

       { heard from
       { run into
       { talked to
Have you { seen   _____ lately?
       { spoken to
       { been in touch
       { with   2

Did you hear (that) _____?   2

How's _____ doing?
How is _____?
How has _____ been?
  Fine.

Great.
Wonderful.
Not too good.
Not very well.   2

Did _____ have anything to say?   1

Have you heard anything about
  _____?
Do you know anything about
  _____?   3

Tell me a little about yourself.   3

What do you want to know?
What would you like to know?
What can I tell you?   3

Is anything { the matter?
         { wrong?
         { bothering you?   12

What's the matter?
What's wrong?
What's the problem?   16

Do you/Would you (by any chance)
  know _____?
Do you/Would you (by any chance)
  happen to know _____?   7

Could you (please/possibly) tell me
  _____?
Do you/Would you (by any chance)
  know _____?
Can you (please) tell me _____?
Would you (possibly/by any chance)
  be able to tell me _____?   11

Did you hear (that) _____?   2

Don't you *work in the bank in the
  High Street?*   1

How is she?
  Fine.
  He/she/they look/s well/okay/fine.   1

Where did you hear that?
How do you know (that)?
Who told you (that)?   2

*School isn't really going to be closed
  tomorrow, is it?*   2

What happened?   3

What's wrong?   7

What makes you say that?
Why do you say that?
Why?
How come? (Am.E.)   6,15,16

Have you by any chance ever
  _____ed?   3

Can you tell me what it's like?   3

Which one is that?   3

People say . . .
They say . . .
People/They tell me . . .
Most people say . . .
Everybody says . . .
Everybody tells me . . .
I hear . . .
I've heard . . .
I'm told . . .   3,12

I heard it on the radio/on TV/on the news.
I saw/read it in the paper. 2

Perhaps
Apparently } you're not aware that
Evidently } _____. 15

Asking for and reporting additional information

What else have you heard?
Have you heard anything else?
Do you know anything else? 3
Can you tell me anything else?
Can you tell me anything more?
What else can you tell me? 3

What did you do next?
What did you do after that?
And then what did you do?
What was the next thing you did? 3

What else would you like to know? 3

As a matter of fact, . . .
In fact, . . . 3

Attracting attention

Excuse me. 8,9,11

Pardon me, . . . (Am.E.) 9

Charles. 11

Certainty/Uncertainty

Enquiring about . . .

Are you sure? 2

Are you positive/certain/sure (about that)? 7,14

Are you (absolutely) sure about that? 14

Is that definite? 14

Expressing certainty

I'm absolutely certain! 2
I'm (absolutely) positive/certain/sure (that _____).
Positively!
Definitely!
Absolutely! (Am.E.) 14

I'm positive/certain/sure.
I'm absolutely positive/certain/sure.
I'm a hundred percent sure.
There's no doubt about it. 7

I know _____.
I'm sure _____.
I'm convinced _____.
I'm certain _____.
I'm positive _____. (Am.E.) 13

I definitely _____.
There's no question (in my mind) _____.
I have no doubt (at all) (that) _____. 14

I'm pretty certain. 14

Expressing uncertainty

I don't know for sure.
I'm not (so) sure.
I'm not (completely/absolutely) certain.
I'm not absolutely positive/certain/sure (about that).
I'm not a hundred percent sure. 2,14

I'm not sure.
I'm not certain.
I don't know yet. 7

I don't think so.
Not as far as I know. 7

I'm not so sure I believe that.
I'm not so sure (about that). 14

I doubt it. 2

Complaining

It's too _____. 4

I was (a little) disappointed.
I wasn't very pleased with it.
It was (a little) disappointing. 4

I'm { annoyed with
upset with
[stronger]
angry with
furious with
mad at
(Am.E.) } _____. 4

He's always
He's constantly } _____ing.
He keeps on 4

I'm tired of _____(ing).
I'm sick of _____(ing).
I'm sick and tired of _____(ing). 4

Complimenting

Expressing compliments

That was { a very good
quite a
[less formal]
some (Am.E.) } _____! 4

I thought it was { excellent.
wonderful.
terrific.
magnificent.
fabulous.
superb. } 4

I (really) like _____.
I love _____. 4

It's very _____.
It's so _____. 4

It's one of the _____est _____s I've ever _____ed. 4

I don't think I've ever seen a _____ better than _____. 4

Responding to compliments

Thanks/Thank you (for saying so).

It's nice/kind of you to say so/that.
I'm glad you like it. 4

Oh, go on!
Oh, come on!
Oh! 4

You're just saying that. 4

Congratulating

That's fantastic!
That's great/wonderful/exciting/ marvellous! 2

Congratulations! 2

I'm very happy to hear that.
I'm very happy for you.
I'm delighted to hear that. 2

Correcting

Giving correction

That isn't exactly/quite right/correct/ true.
That isn't exactly/quite correct.
I think you might be mistaken.
That's just not true! 13

(Actually,) *the bread goes in row FIVE.* 13

That's just not true. *I do like your cooking.* 13

Responding to correction

Thank you for bringing that to my attention.
Thank you for pointing that out.
Thank you for correcting me (on that). (Am.E.) 13

Criticizing

I (do) wish you had (not) _____ed.
As a result of what you _____ed . . . 16

Deduction

You must be _____. 2

_____ must have _____.
_____ probably _____.
_____ most likely _____.
The chances are _____.
I wouldn't be surprised if _____.
[less formal]
I/I'll bet _____. 14

_____ should have _____ed (by now). 14

It looks like _____.
It appears (as if/as though) _____.
It seems (as if/as though) _____. 15

Denying/Admitting

Denying

That's not true.

179

That's/You're wrong.
You're mistaken.
That's just not true.
Certainly not. 13

Admitting

The truth is (that) _____.
The fact of the matter is (that)
_____. 6,15

You see . . .
The reason is . . . 9

I'm afraid _____. 6

I'm afraid you're right.
I'm afraid I have to agree.
I hate to admit it/say it, but you're
right.
I hate to admit it/say it, but it's
true. 13

I (have) made a dreadful/awful/
terrible mistake.
I've been very stupid/foolish.
[less formal]
I (have) (really) goofed! (Am.E.) 15

It's all my fault.
I'm (entirely) to blame.
It's all my doing. 15

Asking for an admission

Why don't you admit it?
You might as well own up.
Admit it! 13

Describing

He's/She's about your height, sort of
heavy, with *curly dark* hair. 3

He's/He's very _____. 3

It's the _____ one with the _____. 3

It's a (very) _____ _____. 3

It's one of the _____est _____s I
know. 3

Directions/Location

Asking for directions

Could you tell me how to get
to _____? 11

Giving directions

Go to _____.
Turn _____.
Walk _____ blocks.
Carry on _____. 11

Disappointment

I was (a little) disappointed.
I wasn't very pleased with it.
I didn't think much of it.
It was (a little) disappointing. 4

I'm (very) disappointed with/in
_____.
I'm very annoyed with _____. 6

Fear/Worry/Anxiety

I'm (getting) (a little)
⎧worried⎫
⎨concerned⎬ about _____.
⎩anxious⎪
⎩nervous⎭ 14

I'm afraid something must have
happened (to him/her/them/it). 14

I wouldn't worry.
I wouldn't be concerned.
Don't worry.
Don't be concerned. (Am.E.) 14

Gratitude

Expressing . . .

Thanks (very much).
Thank you (very much).
I'm most grateful.
I (really) appreciate it. (Am.E.) 8,11

Thanks/Thank you for _____. 12

Thanks a lot. 12

Thanks (for telling me). 9

Thank you for *saying so*.
It's nice of you to *say that/so*. 4

I'm very grateful (to _____). 8

I want to thank _____.
I want to express my gratitude
to _____. 8

I keep forgetting to thank you
for _____. 8

Responding to . . .

Don't mention it.
Not at all.
It was nothing (at all).
You're welcome.
No problem.
Glad to be of help.
I'm glad to do it. 8,11

I'm glad I could help/do it/be of
help.
(It was) my pleasure.
Don't mention it.
[Informal]
Any time. 8

Identifying

My friend *Paul*, my brother
Tom, . . . 1

She's the one who _____. 1

The one *the children gave you*. 3

Intention

Enquiring about . . .

What are you going to do (*next
year*)? 14

What are you doing *this afternoon*? 7

Have you decided _____? 7

Expressing . . .

I'm going to _____.
I'm planning to _____.
I plan to _____.
I intend to _____.
I've decided to _____. 7

I've been thinking of _____ing.
I'm thinking of _____ing.
I've been thinking about _____ing.
I'm thinking about _____ing. 7

I've been meaning to _____ (for a
long time). 7

I've thought about it for a long time.
I've given it a lot of thought.
I've given it a lot of (serious)
consideration. 7

I've decided it's time to do it. 7

I haven't made up my mind yet. 7

I was planning to _____.
I was going to _____.
I intended to _____.
I thought I would _____. 7

I was determined to _____. 7

⎧right away.⎫
I'll _____ ⎨right now.⎬
⎪as soon as I can.⎪
⎩at the first chance I get.⎭ 7

Introducing

Introducing oneself

My name is _____.
I'm _____. 1

Introducing others

Let me introduce (you to) _____.
I'd like to introduce (you to) _____.
I'd like you to meet _____.
[less formal]
This is _____. 1

Invitations

Extending . . .

Would you like to join me?
Do you want to join me?
Would you be interested in joining
me? 7

How would you like to _____?
Would you like to _____?
Do you want to _____?
Would you be interested in
_____ing?
How about _____ing?
Let's _____. 10

Would you (by any chance) be
interested in _____ing?
You wouldn't (by any chance) be
interested in _____ing, would
you? 10

We'd like to invite you (and _____)
round/over for _____.
We'd like to have you (and _____)
round/over for _____.

We'd like you (and _____) to join us
for _____.
We'd like you (and _____) to be our
guest(s) for _____. (Am.E.)   10

Can you come?
Do you think you can come?
Do you think you'd be able to come?
Would you be able to come?
Can you make it?
Do you think you can make it?   10

Please try to come.   10

We hope you'll be able to join us.   10

If you're not busy, . . .
If you're free, . . .
If you don't have any other
plans, . . .   10

Accepting . . .

I'd like to.
I'd love to.
That sounds great/terrific/fun/
wonderful/fun.
That would be great/terrific/
wonderful.
I'd be happy to/glad to.⎫
I'd like that.   ⎬(Am.E.)
That sounds like fun.⎭
[stronger]
I'd be delighted to.   7,10

We'd be ⎧very happy⎫
         ⎪very glad ⎪ to come.
         ⎨pleased   ⎬
         ⎩delighted ⎭   10

We'll be looking forward to it.   10

Thanks/Thank you for ⎧asking.
                     ⎨inviting me.
                     ⎩the invitation.
It's (very) nice of you to invite
me.   10

Declining . . .

I'd love to, but I can't.
I'd love to, but I won't be able to.   10

Leave taking

(You know,) I think I should
⎧be going   ⎫
⎪be on my way   ⎪(now).
⎨be getting on   ⎬
⎪ my way   ⎪
⎩get going (Am.E.)   ⎭
I've (really) got to go now.
I've (really) got to be going now.
I (really) have to go now.
I'd (really) better go now.
I (really) should go now.
I (really) must go now.
I (really) must be going (now).
I have to/I've got to run.
I have to/I've got to get going.   1,16

I should get going, too.   1

I'd love to continue this conversation,
but . . .   10

(I'm afraid) it's getting late.   1

Let's get together soon.

Let's keep in touch.
Let's stay in touch.   1

(I'll) see you soon/later/tomorrow/
next week/ . . .   1

I'll call you.   1

I'll speak to you then.   10

Take care.
Good-bye.
Bye.
Bye-bye.
See you.
Cheerio.
Take it easy.
So long.   (Am.E.)   1,10

Sorry I have to rush off like this.   10

(Well,) I've probably taken up enough
of your time.
(Well,) I know you're a very busy
person.
(Well,) I don't want to waste any
more of your time.   16

I've enjoyed our talk.
It's been a pleasant interview.
It's been a pleasure talking to you.
I've enjoyed talking with you.
(Am.E.)   16

Likes/Dislikes

Enquiring about . . .

How do you like _____?
What do you think of _____?   4

How did you like _____?   4

Did you like _____?   4

Don't you like _____?   4

Expressing likes

I like _____.
I love _____.   4

Expressing dislikes

I don't (really) like/enjoy _____ very
much.
I don't (particularly) care for _____.
I'm not (really) keen on _____.
[stronger]
I hate _____.   4

Meeting and greeting

Hello.
[less formal]
Hi.
[more formal]
How do you do?   1

(I'm) glad to meet you.
(I'm) pleased to meet you.
(It's) nice to meet you.
(It's) nice meeting you.   (Am.E.)
(I'm) happy to meet you.   1

How are you?
[less formal]

How are things?
How's it going?
How are you doing? (Am.E.)
Fine (thank you/thanks).
All right.
Okay.
Not bad.   1

Neutrality

Whenever _____ is fine with me.
(Whoever . . . Whatever . . . However
. . . Whichever . . . Wherever . . .)   5

It makes no difference (to me).
It doesn't matter (to me).
It's all the same to me.
I don't mind.
I don't feel strongly about it (one
way or the other).   5

It doesn't matter to me whether you
_____ or not.   5

It's (entirely) up to you.
It's (entirely) your decision.
It's for you to decide.   5

Obligations

Expressing . . .

I have to _____.
I've got to _____.
I'm supposed to _____.
I must _____.   1,10,11

I'm expected to _____.   10

You're supposed to _____.
You're required to _____.
You're expected to _____.
You need to _____.
You have to _____.
You've got to _____.
You must _____.
It's necessary (for you) to _____.
It's required that you _____.
(Am.E.)   16

It's required/necessary/essential/
compulsory/mandatory. (Am.E.)   16

_____ is insisting that I _____.
_____ is wanting me to _____.
[stronger]
_____ is making me _____.
_____ is forcing me to _____.   7

I was supposed to _____.
I said I would _____.
I had promised to _____.
I had promised you I would
_____.   6

I don't think I can get out of it.   10

I'm tied up on _____.
I've got an appointment on
_____.   10

I didn't know that was required/
compulsory/necessary/essential/
mandatory. (Am.E.)   16

You were counting/depending on me
to _____.
You were counting/depending on my
_____ing.
You had expected me to _____.   6

We feel obliged to _____.
We feel compelled to _____.
We feel we must _____.
We feel we have to _____.
We feel we should _____. 16

Offering to do something

Would you like me to _____?
I'll _____, if you'd like.
I'll/I'd be happy/glad to _____,
 (if you'd like). 8

Let me (_____). 8

Can I take a message?
Can I give him/her a message?
Would you like to leave a message
 (for him/her)? 11

Offering to help

Making an offer

(Do you) want any help?
(Do you) need any help?
(Do you) want a hand?
(Do you) need a hand?
Can I help?
Can I give you a hand? 8

Would you like me to help you
 _____?
Do you want me to help you _____?
I'd be glad/happy to help you _____,
 (if you'd like).
Let me help you _____.
Would you like any help _____ing?
Would you like me to give you a
 hand _____ing? 8

Can I do anything to help?
Is there anything I can do to help?
Can I help? 8

I'd be glad/happy to give you a hand.
I'd be glad/happy to lend a hand.
I'd be glad/happy to help. 8

Let me give you a hand.
I'm happy to lend a hand. 8

Let me _____.
I'll _____.
Allow me to _____. (Am.E.) 8

Can I help you?
Can I assist you? 8

Is there anything/something particular
 I can help you find?
Is there anything/something you're
 looking for in particular? 8

Is there anything else I can help
 you with? 8

Responding to an offer

If you don't mind.
If you wouldn't mind.
If it's no trouble. 8

I don't want to {
 trouble you.
 bother you.
 inconvenience you.
 put you to any
  trouble.
 put you out. 8

Don't worry about it.
That's okay/all right. 8

Permission

Asking for . . .

Can/Could I (possibly) _____?
Can/Could I please _____?
May I (please) _____?
Is it all right/okay (with you) if I
 _____?
Would it be possible for me to
 _____?
I'd like to _____, if that's all right/
 okay (with you).
Would it be all right/okay (with you)
 if I _____ed? 9

Would you mind/object if I _____ed?
Would it bother you if I _____ed?
Do you mind if I _____? 9

Granting . . .

Of course.
Certainly.
By all means.
It's all right/okay with me.
Yes.
Sure. (Am.E.) 9

No, I wouldn't mind.
No, I don't mind.
(No,) of course not.
(No,) not at all.
No, it's all right/fine/okay with me.
No. 9

Go ahead.
Be my guest. 9

I think so.
I suppose so.
I don't see (any reason) why not. 9

If you want to _____, it's
 {
 fine
 all right } with/by me.
 okay
 9

Denying . . .

I'd rather you didn't.
I'd prefer it if you didn't/wouldn't.
I'd prefer you not to. 9

_____ing isn't allowed.
You mustn't _____ (under any
 circumstances).
We don't allow anyone to _____.
You're not supposed to _____.
You may not _____ (without
 permission). 9

That's out of the question. 9

I can't do that without
 {
 permission from
 the permission of
 the approval of
 the consent of
 the agreement of
 an authorization from
 _____. (Am.E.) 9

Enquiring about permissibility

Is _____ing allowed/permitted?

Is it okay to _____?
Is it all right to _____?
Are you allowed to _____?
Are people allowed to _____?
Do they allow _____ing?
Do they allow people to _____?
Is one allowed to _____? 9

Indicating permissibility

I don't think _____ing is allowed.
I don't think you're allowed to
 _____.
I don't think people are allowed
 to _____.
I don't think they allow people to
 _____.
I don't think they allow you to
 _____. 9

Yes, _____ _____.
[less certain]
I think so.
I believe so.
Yes, as far as I know. 9

No, _____ _____.
[less certain]
I don't think so.
I don't believe so.
Not as far as I know. 9

Persuading/Insisting

I mean it!
I'm (really/quite) serious.
I'm being perfectly honest with
 you. 4

Listen!
Look!
(No,) really!
(No,) I mean it!
(No,) honestly!
(Oh,) come on! 8,9,13

I insist. 8

Let me, for a change.
Let me, for once. 8

There's no sense in _____ing.
There's no reason (for you) to _____.
You don't have to _____.
You shouldn't have to _____. 8

Possibility/Impossibility

Enquiring about . . .

What's the possibility of _____? 14

Expressing possibility

I might _____.
I may _____.
I thought I might _____.
I thought I'd _____.
Perhaps I'll _____.
Maybe I'll _____. 7,14

Perhaps. 14

You might _____.
You could (possibly) _____.
You could/would run the risk of
 _____ing.
There's a chance you might/could
 _____. 12

182

_____ might have _____ed.
_____ may have _____ed.   14

Expressing impossibility

There's no chance that _____.
There's no possibility (that) _____.
[less formal]
There's no way (that) _____.
(Am.E.)   14

Preference

Enquiring about . . .

Would you {prefer _____?
rather have _____?
like _____?   5

Would you like to
Would you prefer
to
Would you rather   } _____ (or _____)?
Would you care to   5

How would you like it?   5

Do you have any strong feelings
about it?
Do you have any feelings about it
one way or another?
Do you care one way or another?
Do you have a preference/any
preferences?   5

Expressing . . .

I'd prefer _____.
I'd rather have _____.
I'd like _____.   5

I'd prefer to _____.
I'd rather _____.
I'd like to _____.
I'd much rather _____.   5
I'd prefer not to _____.   5

I feel strongly about _____ing.   5

If you'd rather I didn't _____, I
won't.   5

Probability/Improbability

Enquiring about . . .

What are the chances of _____?
What do you think the chances are
of _____?
What's the likelihood of _____?
What's the possibility of _____?   14

Is there a good/much chance
_____?   14

Expressing probability

I'll probably _____.
I'm pretty sure I'll _____.
The chances are I'll _____.
I guess I'll _____.
I suppose I'll _____.
I'll most likely _____. (Am.E.)   7,14

That's most probably . . .
In all probability . . .   14

If I had to choose between _____ and
_____, I'd probably _____.   14

It should
It ought to
It'll probably
In all probability it'll   } *arrive any minute now.*
The chances are it'll
It'll most likely (Am.E.)   14

Expressing improbability

The chances are probably not very
high.
It/That isn't very likely.
[less formal]
The chances are pretty slim.   14

There's not much chance of that
happening.
I doubt if that would/could/will
happen.
I don't think that will happen.
That's not likely to happen.
That's not very likely.   14

Promising

Asking for a promise

Can I {rely on
depend on   } you to _____?   6
count on

Can I {depend on
count on
rely on   } that?   6
be sure of

Promise?   7

Making a promise

Promise.
I promise I'll _____.
I promise to _____.   6

I promise (you) _____.
I guarantee _____.
I can assure you _____.
I give you my word _____.
You can be sure _____.   6

Absolutely.
Definitely.
Of course.   6

You can {rely on
depend on   } me.
count on   6

I won't let you down.
I won't disappoint you.   6

Regret

It's a shame (that) _____.
It's a pity (that) _____.
(It's) too bad (that) _____.
I'm disappointed (that) _____.
It's disappointing (that) _____.
(Am.E.)   15

I regret _____ing.
I regret (that) I _____.
I'm sorry about _____ing.
I'm sorry (that) I _____.   15

I could kick myself!
I'm an idiot/a fool!
[stronger]
I could shoot myself! (Am.E.)   15

Remembering/Forgetting

Enquiring about . . .

Did you (happen to) remember to
_____?
You didn't (by any chance) remember
to _____, did you?   7

Indicating . . .

You remember.   3

Oh, that one.   3

I forgot (all about it).
I completely/clean forgot.
It (completely) slipped my mind.
It went (clean) out of my mind.   7

I forgot to _____.
I've been meaning to _____.   15

Requests

Direct, polite

Please _____.
Could you (please) _____?
Will you (please) _____?   11

Would you (please) _____?
I'd like you to _____.
I wish you would _____.   11

Could you do me a favour?
Could I ask you a favour?
Could you do a favour for me?   11

Could I ask you to _____?   9

Would you please ask/tell _____
to _____?   11

Direct, more polite

Could you possibly _____?
Could you (please) _____?
Could I (possibly) ask you to _____?
Would you mind _____ing?
Would you be willing to _____?
Do you think you'd be able to _____?
I wonder if you could (possibly)
_____.   3,11

Would you mind
Would it bother you   } if I _____ed?
Would it disturb you

Less direct, very polite

Would you be kind enough to _____?
Would you mind if I asked you to
_____?   11

Responding to requests

Okay.
All right.
Certainly.
Of course.
I'd be glad/happy to.
Sure. (Am.E.)   11

No, I wouldn't mind.
No, of course not.
No, not at all.

No problem.
No trouble at all. 11

Satisfaction/Dissatisfaction

Enquiring about ...

How do you like _____?
What do you think of _____? 4

How are you enjoying _____? 15

How did you like _____? 4

Did you (really) like it? 4

Are you { satisfied / happy / pleased } with it? 4

Is it _____ enough? 4

What seems to be the problem (with it)?
What seems to be the matter (with it)?
What's the problem/matter/wrong (with it)? 4

Expressing satisfaction

It's { fine. / very nice. / perfect. } 4

It's just what I { had in mind. / wanted. / was looking for. } 4

I wouldn't want it any _____er. 4

Expressing dissatisfaction

It's too _____. 4

I'm not enjoying _____ (at all). 15

I really { expected it to be / thought it would be / hoped it would be } _____er. 4

It wasn't as _____ as I thought it would be. 4

Surprise/Disbelief

Assistant manager?!
1:30?! Already?!
They're going to make the park across the street into a cark park?! 1,2

School isn't really going to be closed tomorrow, is it? 2

I didn't realize _____. 1

Oh? 9

You're joking!
I don't/can't believe it.
Oh, come on!
No!
That can't be!
You must be joking.
You're kidding! }
No kidding! } (Am.E.) 2

Really?
Good heavens!
My word!
Gee! }
Boy! } (Am.E.)
Wow! } 7

Well, now!
Goodness (me)!
Good gracious!
Good heavens!
(Well,) how about that!
(Well,) what do you know! }
(Well,) how do you like that! } (Am.E.)
Isn't that something! } 9

Sympathizing

That's awful!
That's a shame/a pity!
What a shame/a pity!
That's terrible!
That's too bad. (Am.E.) 2,6,15

That's terrible/awful/dreadful!
How terrible/awful/dreadful! 15

I'm (very) sorry to hear (about) that.
I'm (very/so) sorry. 2,15

Want/Desire

Enquiring about ...

When do you want to _____?
Who would you like to _____?
What would you like to do?
How would you like me to _____?
Which _____ would you rather _____?
Where do you want _____ to _____? 5

What do you want to do today? 12

Expressing ...

I'd like _____.
I'll have _____.
I want _____. 5

I (really) don't feel like _____ing.

I'm not (really) in the mood for _____ing. 5,12

I'd (really) prefer not to _____. 5

_____ wants me to _____. 5

Warning

(You'd better) *get out of the way!*
(You'd better) *stay away from the* _____!
(You'd better) keep clear of the _____!
You'd better not _____!
Don't _____! 12

If you don't (_____), _____. 12

Be careful!
Look out!
Watch out! 12

You might _____. 12

You'll be disappointed.
You'll be sorry.
You'll regret it. 14

Willingness

Enquiring about ...

Would you be willing to ...?
Would you be kind enough to ...?
Would you mind _____ing? 11

Expressing ...

Of course.
All right.
I'd be glad/happy to.
Sure. (Am.E.)
[informal]
Okay. 11

No, I wouldn't (mind).
Not at all.
[informal]
No problem. 11

I'll do it { right away / straight away / at once / immediately } 11

Wish/Hope

I wish *it were cheaper.* 15

I wish I could _____.
If only I could _____. 15

I was hoping _____. 15

Conversation strategies

Asking for repetition

Excuse me. 16

I didn't hear what you said.

I didn't hear you.
I didn't catch what you said.
I didn't quite catch that.
What did you say?
I beg your pardon.

Pardon me? (Am.E.) 16
Eh?
What?
[more polite]
Sorry?

Excuse me?
Pardon (me)? } (Am.E.)   12

(Sorry,) I didn't hear you.   11

What did you ask me to do?
What did you say?
What was that?   11

WHEN do you want me to _____?
WHEN should I _____?
WHEN did you tell me to _____?   16

Have I had it what?!   16

Huh?   12

Checking and indicating understanding

Checking another person's understanding

(Have you) got that?
Do you follow me?
Okay?   11

Do you think you've got it now?   11

Checking one's own understanding

Let me see.
Let me see if I understand.
Let me see if I've got that (right).   11

This Saturday evening?
7:00?
Change seats?
'Tooth-brite'?
Any minute now?   10,11,12,14

Indicating understanding

(Now) { I understand.
I see.
I follow you.
[informal]
I get you/it.   16

Uh-huh.
Um-hmm.
Yes.
(That's) right.   11

Clarification

Asking for clarification

Do you mean (to say) _____?
Are you saying _____?
Does that mean _____?   15

[less direct]
I'm afraid I don't follow you.
I'm not really sure what you're getting at.
I'm afraid I'm not with you.
I'm not quite clear (as to) what you mean (by that).
I'm afraid I'm not following you. (Am.E.)

[more direct]
What do you mean (by that)?
What does that mean?   16

Giving clarification

Let me put it this way: ...
Let me put it another way: ...
What I'm (really) saying is ...
What I'm trying to say is ...
What I mean is ...
What I'm getting at is ...
In other words ...   16

Directing/Redirecting a conversation

(Oh,) by the way/bye, ...
(Oh,) incidentally, ...   1,16

(Oh,) before I forget, ...
I don't mean to change the subject, but ...   16

(Now) as I was saying, ...
(Now) to get back to what I was saying, ...
(Now) to get back to what we were talking about, ...   16

Focusing attention

As a matter of fact, ...
In fact, ...   3

If you ask me, ...
In my opinion, ...
As far as I'm concerned, ...
I personally think ...
As I see it, ...
The way I see it ...   3,13,16

The thing to keep in mind is ...   16

In fact, ...
To tell the truth, ...   14

What it boils down to is that ...
The fact of the matter is that ...
As it turned out, ...   7

Hesitating

Hmm.   9,12,14

Er ...   5,14

Well, er, ...   3

Well ...   6,12,14

Let me see ...
Let's see ...
(Well,) let's see ...
Let's see now ...   3,5,9,12

Let me think (for a minute).   9

I think ...
I guess ... (Am.E.)   5

Well, I don't know ...   14

I don't know where to begin.
I don't know where to start.
I don't know what to say.   3

Initiating a conversation

Excuse me, but ...
Pardon me, but ... (Am.E.)   1

I don't think we've met.   1

Don't I know you from somewhere?   1

(Hello). { Can/Could I (please) speak to _____?
I'd like to speak to _____ (please), (if he's/she's there).
Is _____ there?   11

Hello! It's me!   7

Hi! It's me again!   7

Well, if it isn't _____!   7

Initiating a topic

You know, ...   7,8,16

You know *what I wish?*   15

I have some good/bad news.   2

Have you heard the news?   2

Guess { who
what } _____!

You won't believe { who
what } _____!   1

I've been meaning to ask you ...   14,15

I keep forgetting to ask you ...
I keep meaning to ask you ...   15

(You know,) I've been thinking ...   15

Don't you think (that) _____?
Wouldn't you say (that) _____?
Wouldn't you agree (that) _____?   13

I hate to say this ... but ...   16

(Now,) regarding _____, ...
(Now,) regarding the issue of _____, ...
(Now,) as far as _____ is concerned, ...   16

You seem troubled/upset.
You don't seem to be yourself today.   12

Let me tell you about _____.
Let me explain _____.   16

Interrupting

Excuse me for interrupting, (but) ...   16

INDEX OF FUNCTIONS AND CONVERSATION STRATEGIES

Note References are to lesson units not page numbers.

INDEX OF GRAMMATICAL STRUCTURES

Note References are to lesson units not page numbers.